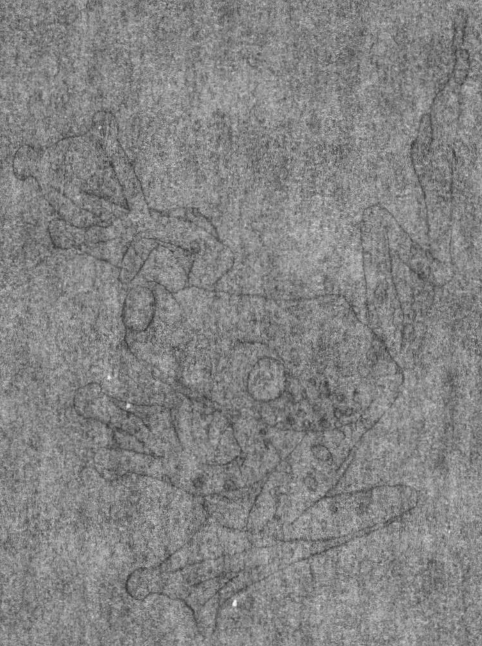

PAINTINGS & WATERCOLORS

by:

ALEXIS ROCKMAN.

ENVISIONING:

WALLACE'S LINE.

Facets of Alfred Russel Wallace in Alexis Rockman's artworks,

by JEAN-CHRISTOPHE CASTELLI.

Published by:

BALDWIN GALLERY

209 SOUTH GALENA STREET

ASPEN, COLORADO 81611.

I thought of the long ages of the past, during which the successive generations of this little creature had run their course—year by year being born, and living and dying amid these dark and gloomy woods, with no intelligent eye to gaze upon their loveliness; to all appearance such a wanton waste of beauty. Such ideas excite a feeling of melancholy. It seems sad that on the one hand such exquisite creatures should live out their lives and exhibit their charms only in these wild inhospitable regions, doomed for ages yet to come to hopeless barbarism; while, on the other hand, should civilized man ever reach these distant lands, and bring moral, intellectual, and physical light into the recesses of these virgin forests, we may be sure that he will so disturb the nicely-balanced relations of organic and inorganic nature as to cause the disappearance, and finally the extinction, of these very beings whose wonderful structure and beauty he alone is fitted to appreciate and enjoy. This consideration must surely tell us that all living things were not made for man. Many of them have no relation to him. The cycle of their existence has gone on independently of his, and is disturbed or broken by every advance in man's intellectual development; and their happiness and enjoyments, their loves and hates, their struggles for existence, their vigorous life and early death, would seem to be immediately related to their own well-being and perpetuation alone, limited only by the equal well-being and perpetuation of the numberless other organisms with which each is more or less intimately connected.

ALFRED RUSSEL WALLACE, *THE MALAY ARCHIPELAGO*, 1869.

Alfred Russel Wallace was an ambitious, self-taught scientist and explorer from a poor background, and one of the great, unsung heroes of 19th century science. Ambition and financial need led Wallace to wide-ranging travels in the Amazon basin and Indonesia, and through the very Victorian practice of collecting and preserving 'specimens', he was able to discover a multitude of species and habitats. In a delirious, yellow fever-induced dream on a remote Indonesian island, Wallace formulated one of the most revolutionary ideas in the history of science—Natural Selection. He sent his discovery to his acquaintance Charles Darwin, who had already independently come up with the same concept. Wallace's letter spurred the older scientist to write On The Origin of Species, *and needless to say, Wallace never received the credit he deserved. These paintings explore and celebrate Wallace's life and work, and speculate on how he saw nature, a vision which led to his profound insights into the natural world and our place in it.*

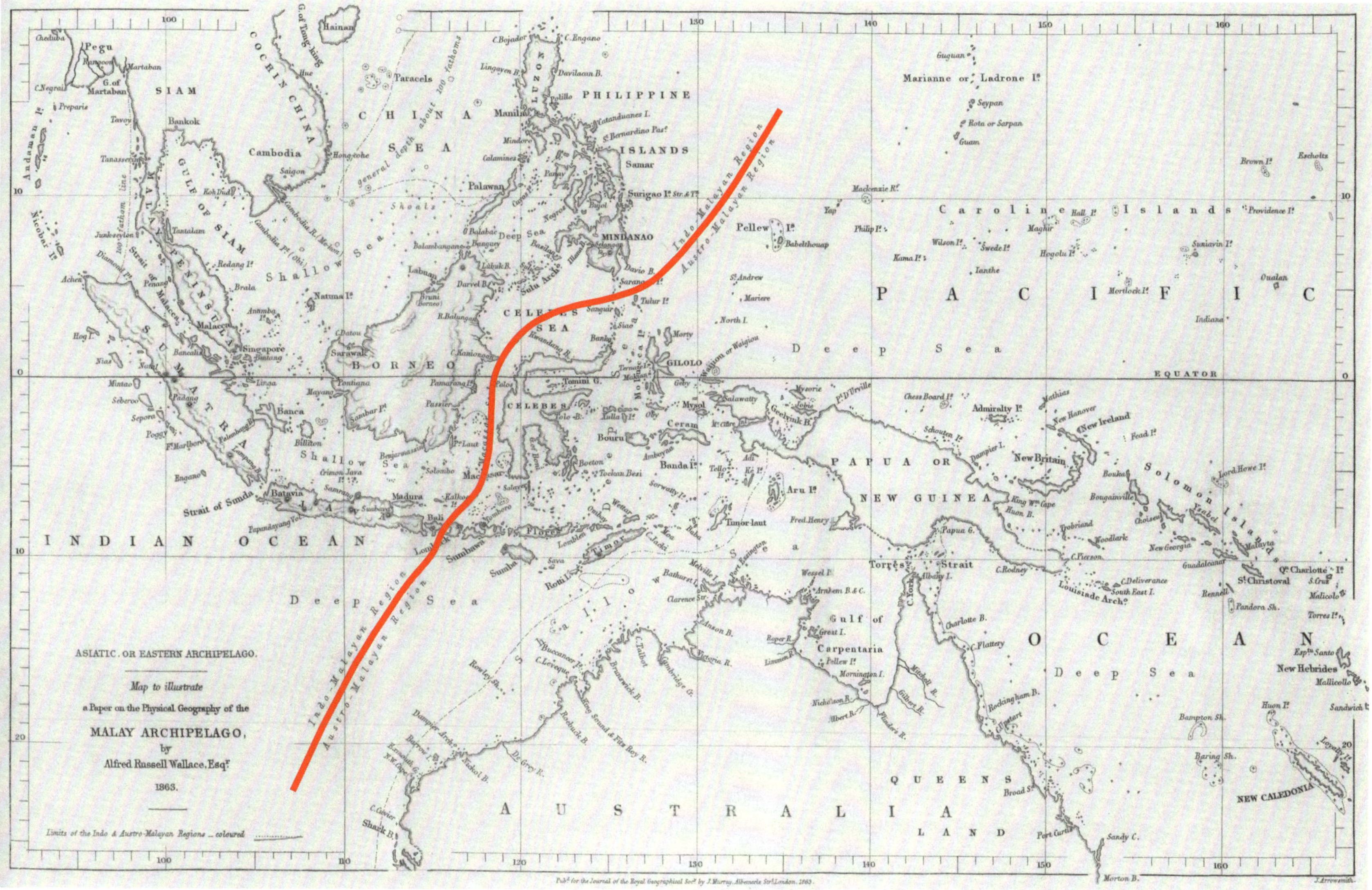

Wallace's Line, first proposed in 1859, delineates flora and fauna of Asia (west of the line), and Australasia (east of the line).

LEAVING.

With the help of a curious and colorful flightless cassowary bird, we draw back the heavy Victorian curtain that separates us from Alfred Russel Wallace, hoping to catch a glimpse of the celebrated yet enigmatic biologist and explorer. Wallace was one of the greatest wildlife collectors of the 19th century, so you might expect a cabinet of curiosities behind the red velvet, lined with glass cases and heavy oak drawers containing beetles and butterflies, taxidermied birds in all their exotically-plumed glory, and many other preserved animals. Instead, there is a river, framed by lush, undifferentiated jungle; and in the foreground, a rifle, net, crate, bag, hat, boat—the tools of Wallace's traveling trade. Time to push off into the unknown, first to find yourself, perhaps, reflected in the mirror-smooth water—and then to find something else, some undiscovered marvel. From his early youth as an apprentice land surveyor in Wales and throughout his long life, Wallace was ever departing: seeking the next job, the next butterfly, the next bend in the Amazon river, the next Indonesian island... And when he finally returned to England for good, his exploring days at an end, Wallace continued to beat against the current in search of the next idea, the ever-shifting answer to the question: who in this world are we?

DEPARTURE, 2018, OIL ON DIBOND, 44 X 56 IN.

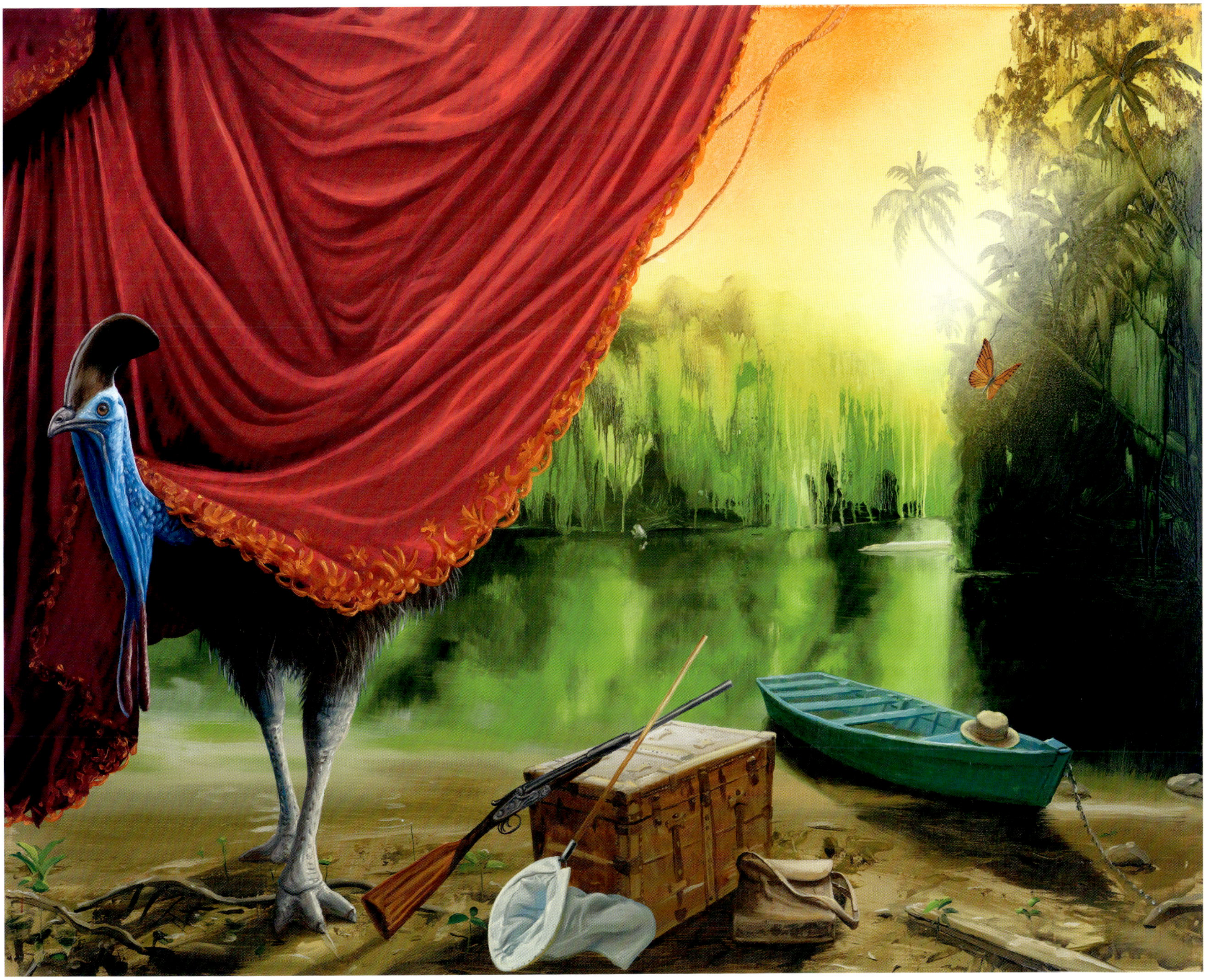

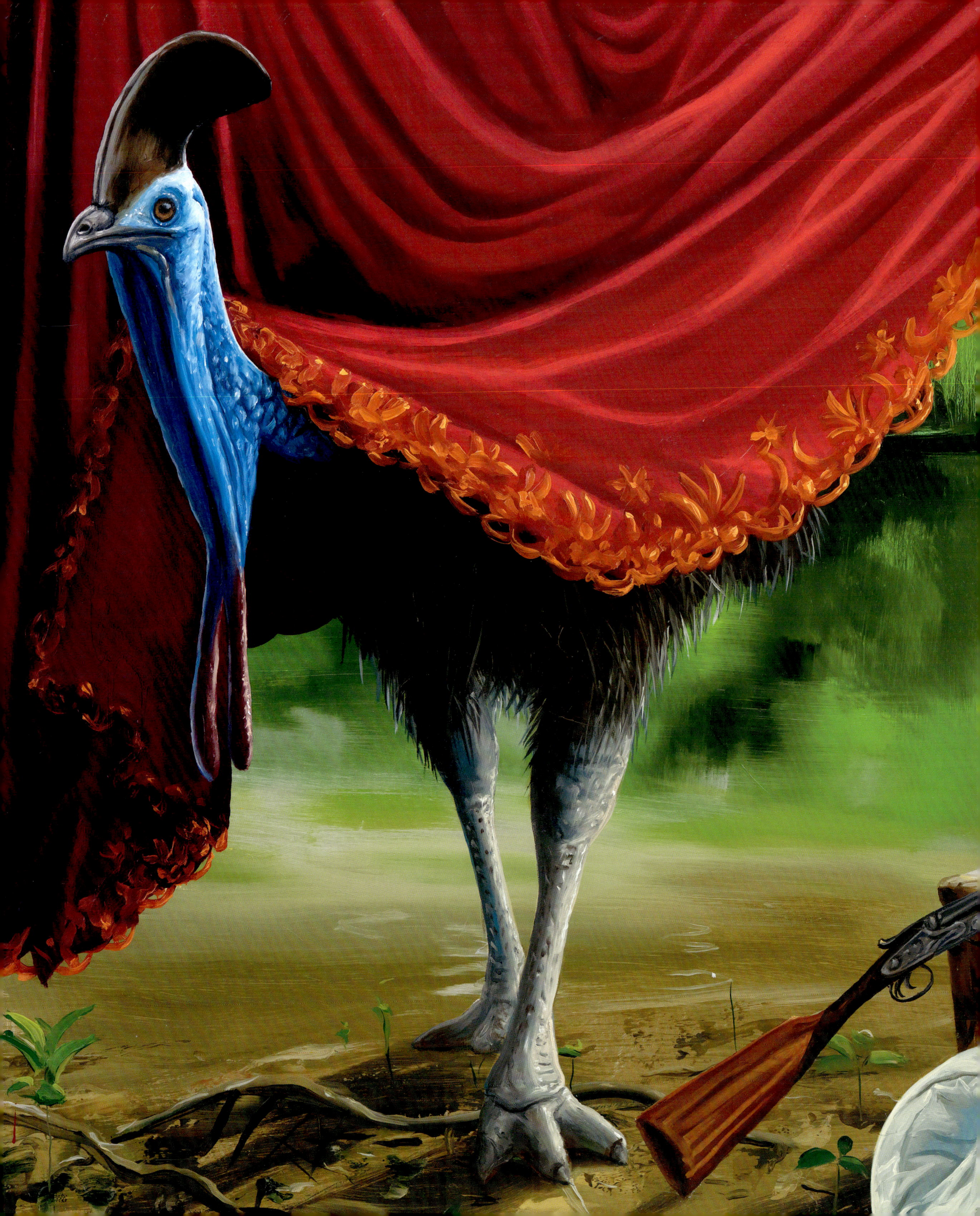

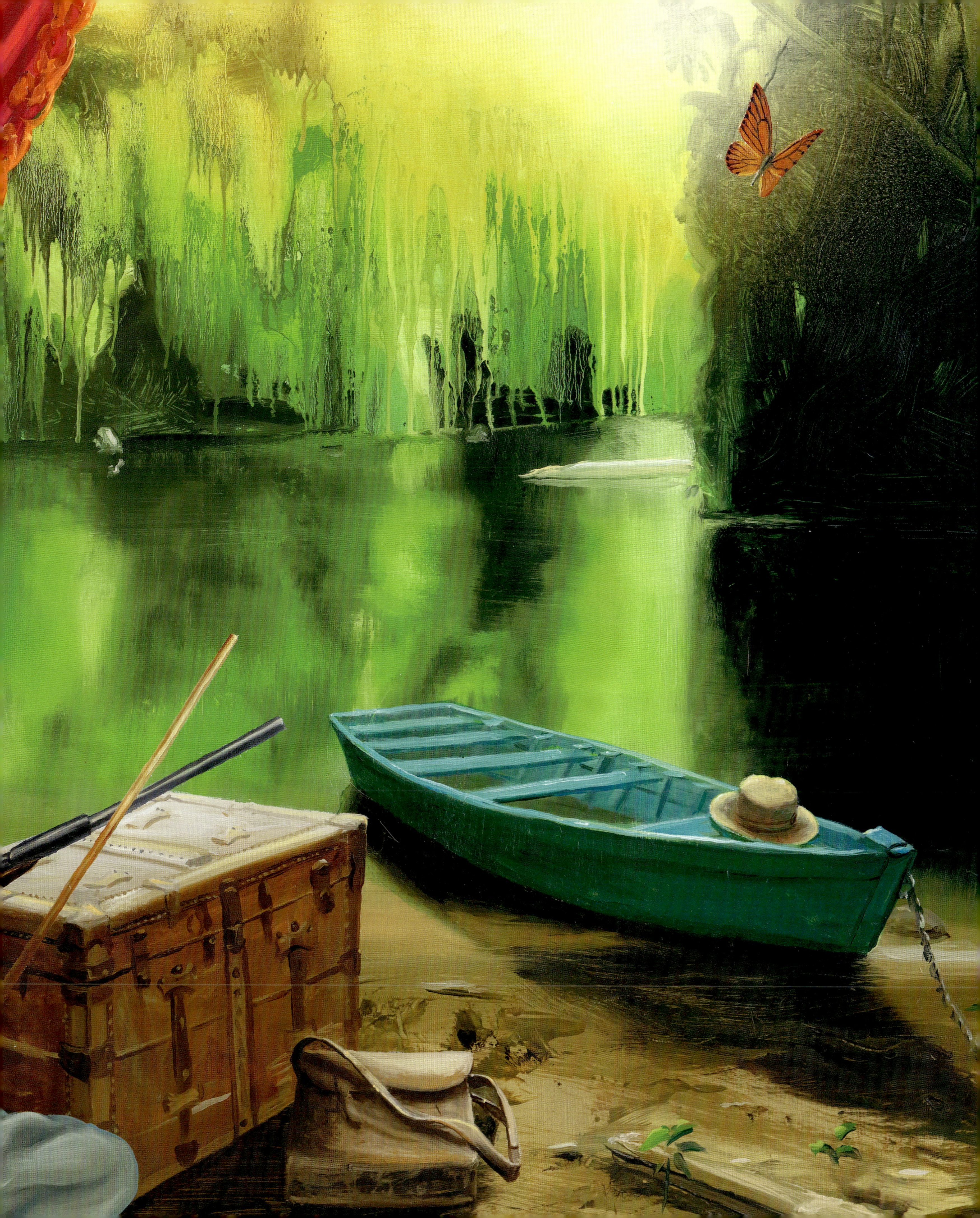

LOSS.

(*The Window* and *The Circle of Life*)

A modest English country church, surrounded by gravestones and grieving angels. 22-year-old Alfred Russel Wallace might be found inside, sitting through the funeral service for his older brother and mentor, William, who died in 1845, consumed by fever as the bird in the windowframe of their modest cottage is consumed by the spider. The minister inside the church preaches eternal life; but on the edge of William's freshly-dug grave, religion's consoling narrative is displaced by a death that is at once trivial and universal—the body of a gray squirrel, food for bacteria and carrion beetles. In nature, the place of the angels is filled by insects, and mourning becomes mulch; bodies nourish the earth, which brings forth plants that, in turn, nourish new bodies. Lilies, those hot-house symbols of death, wilt before the wild flowers; creation gives way to evolution and biography bends into a circle: the circle of life.

THE WINDOW, 2018, OIL ON DIBOND, 18 X 24 IN.

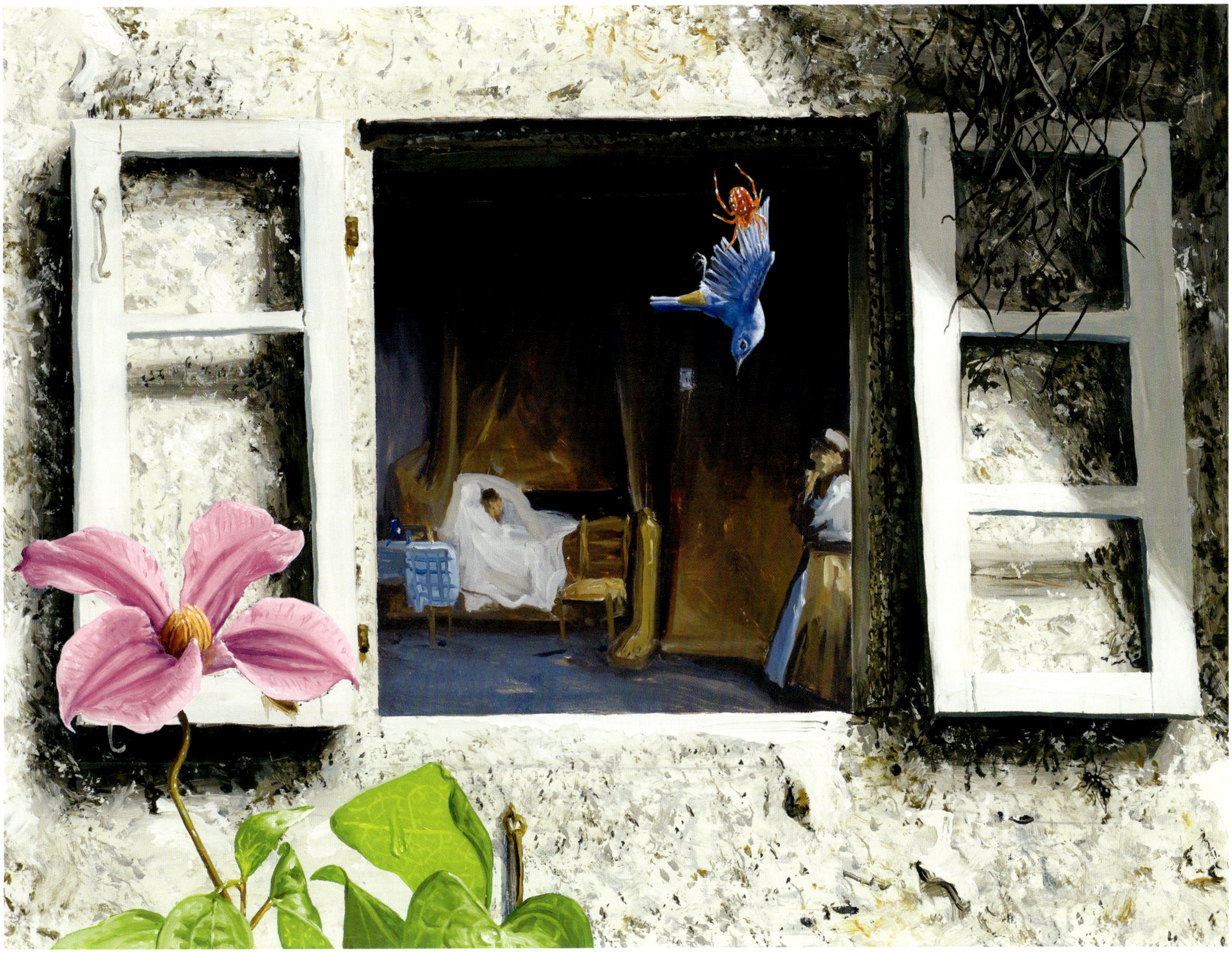

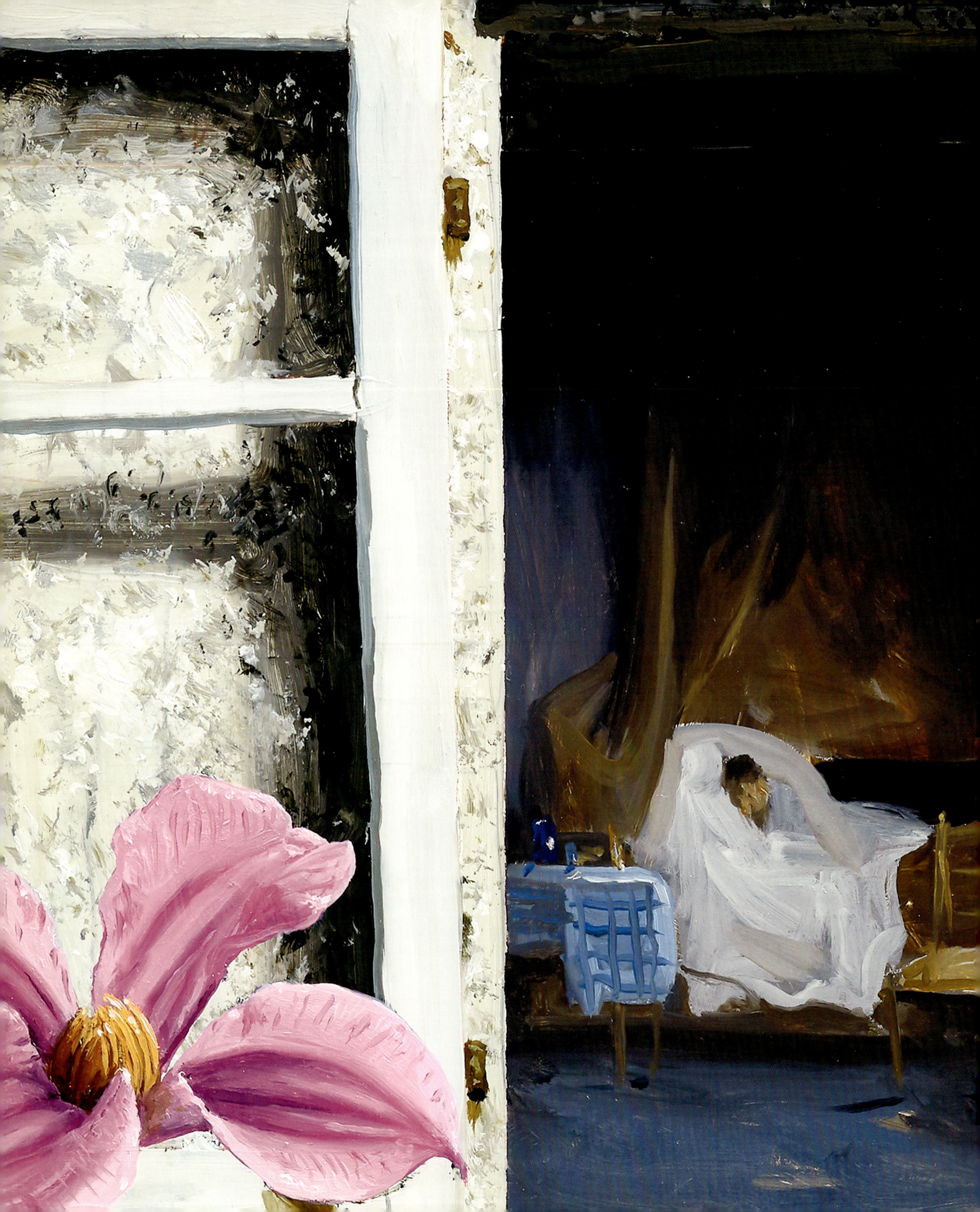

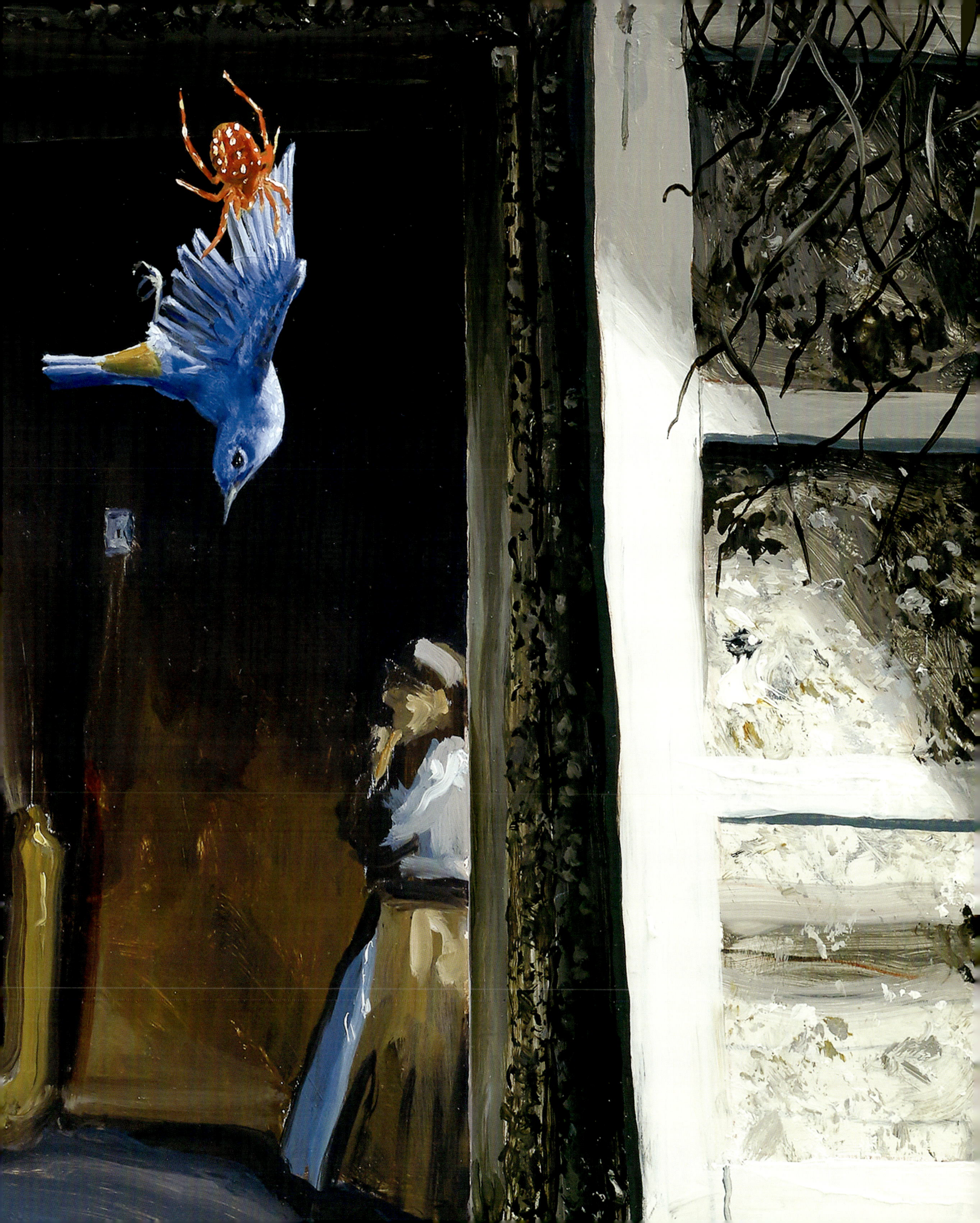

THE CIRCLE OF LIFE, 2017, OIL ON DIBOND, 56 X 44 IN.

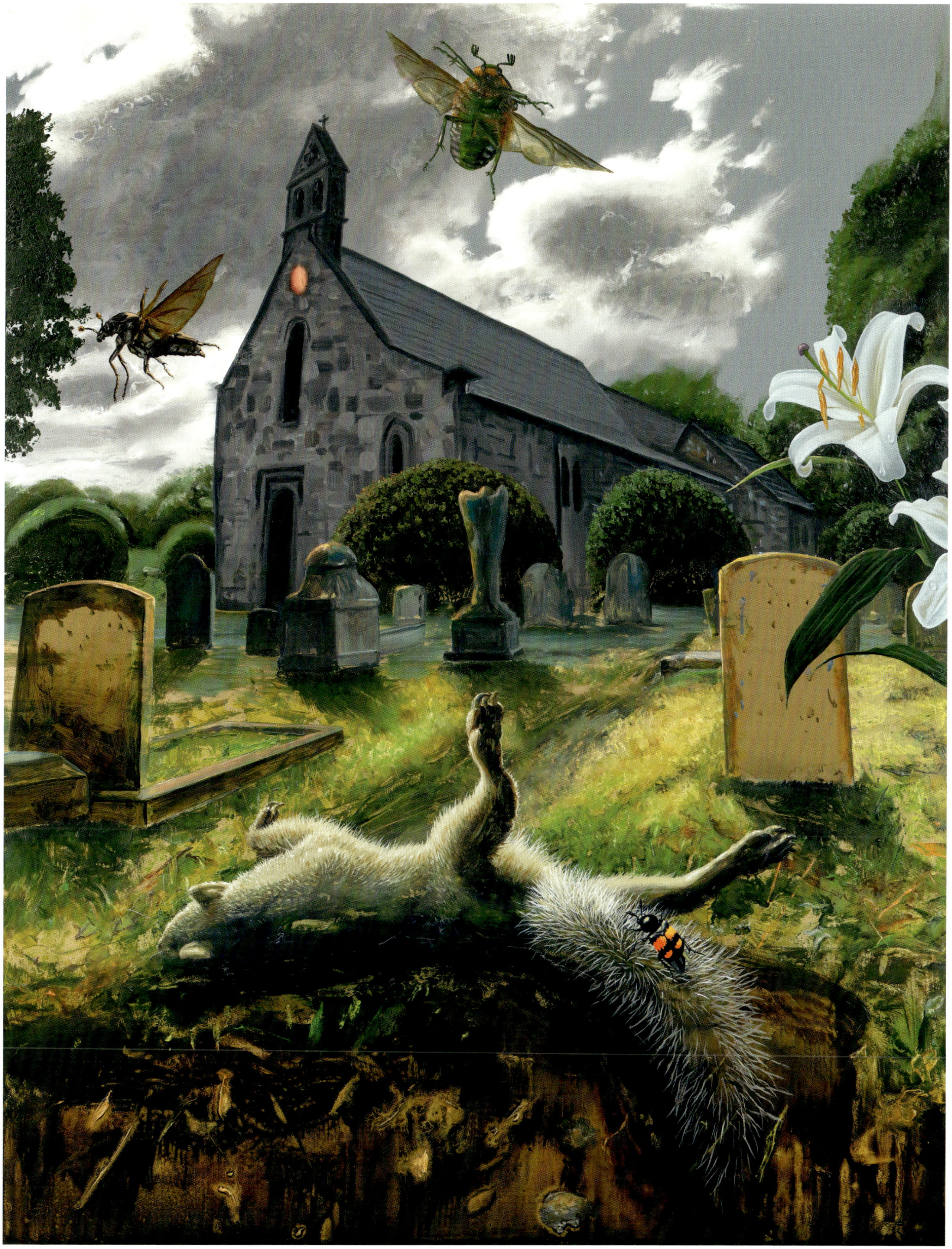

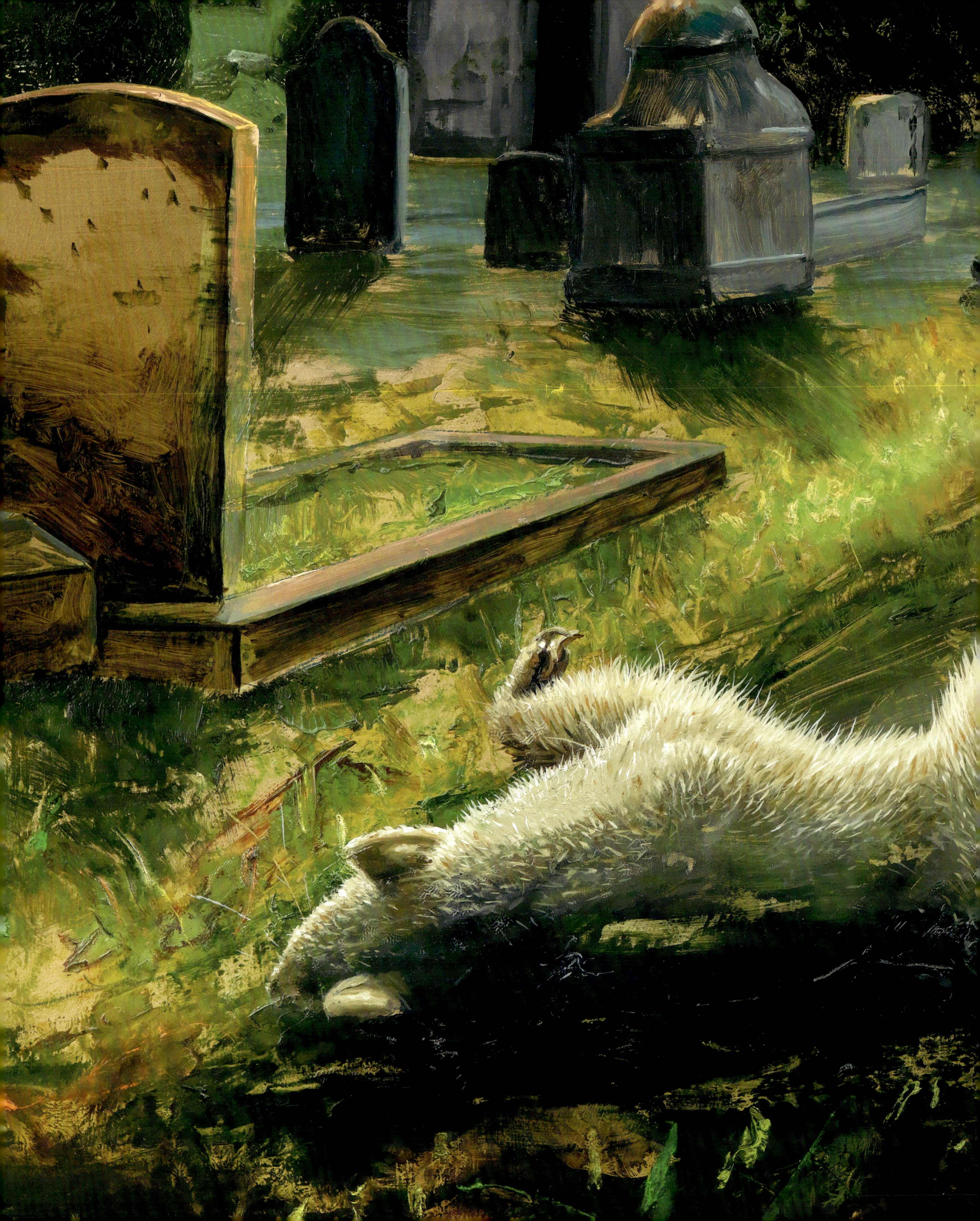

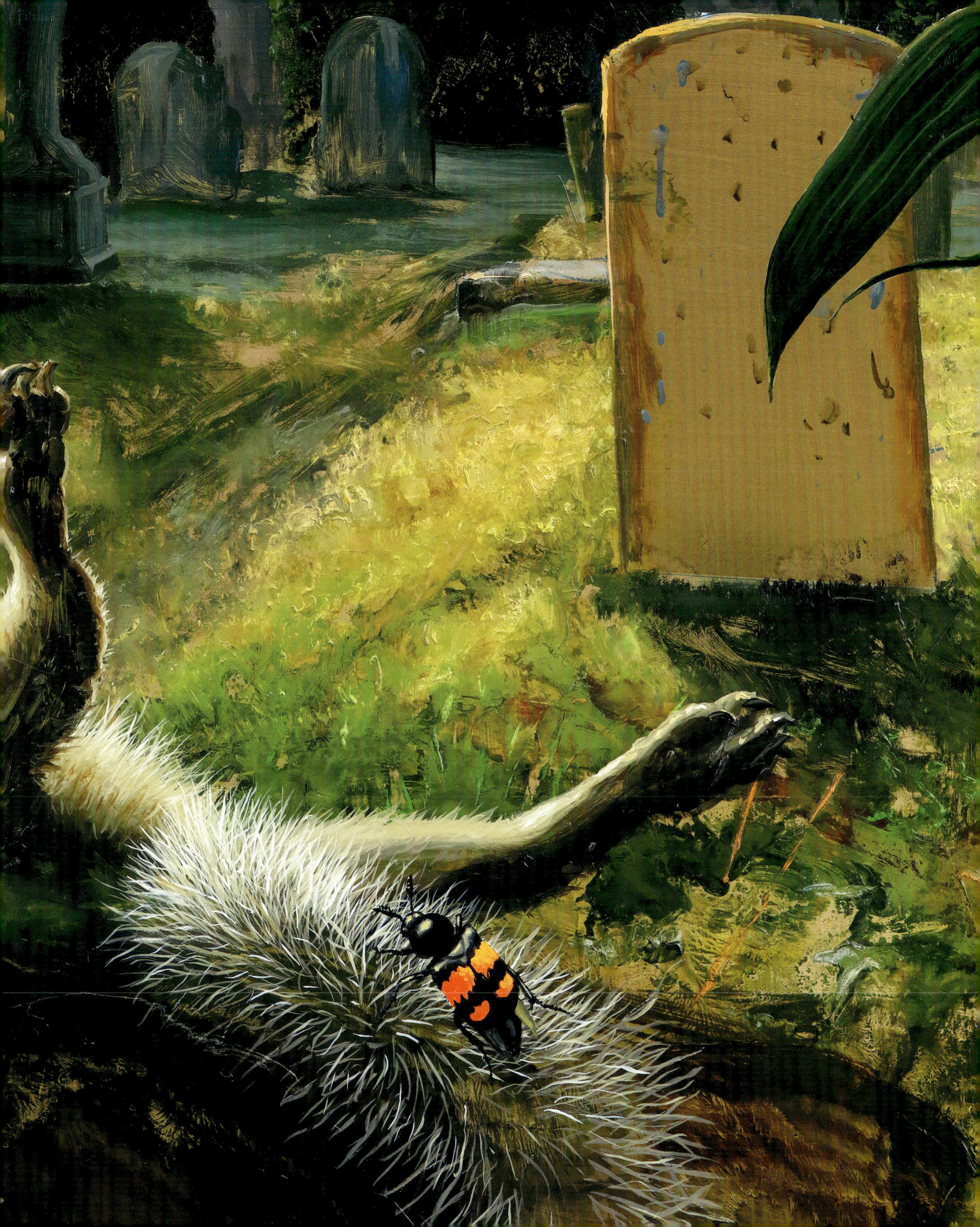

SHIPWRECK.

Imagine spending more than four years (1848–1852) exploring the rivers of the South American Amazon on your first, self-financed scientific expedition, four years of astonishing discoveries and wracking tropical fevers—hundreds of thousands of specimens (many new to science) carefully packed in the hold of a ship, the brig Helen, now headed back to England. Now imagine waking up, as Alfred Russel Wallace did one morning in August, to find the ship on fire, and having to leave everything—*everything*—behind. A few live specimens, macaws, fly off into nowhere, like your dream giving up its brightly-colored ghost. The rest goes down, down to the bottom. You end up drifting at sea for ten days, staring into the depths that have swallowed up your future as a professional scientist. But then, one day, you raise your eyes to the horizon. No land is visible, nor rescue yet, but maybe it's enough to start thinking: to begin again.

THE SINKING OF THE BRIG HELEN, 2017, OIL ON DIBOND, 56 X 44 IN.

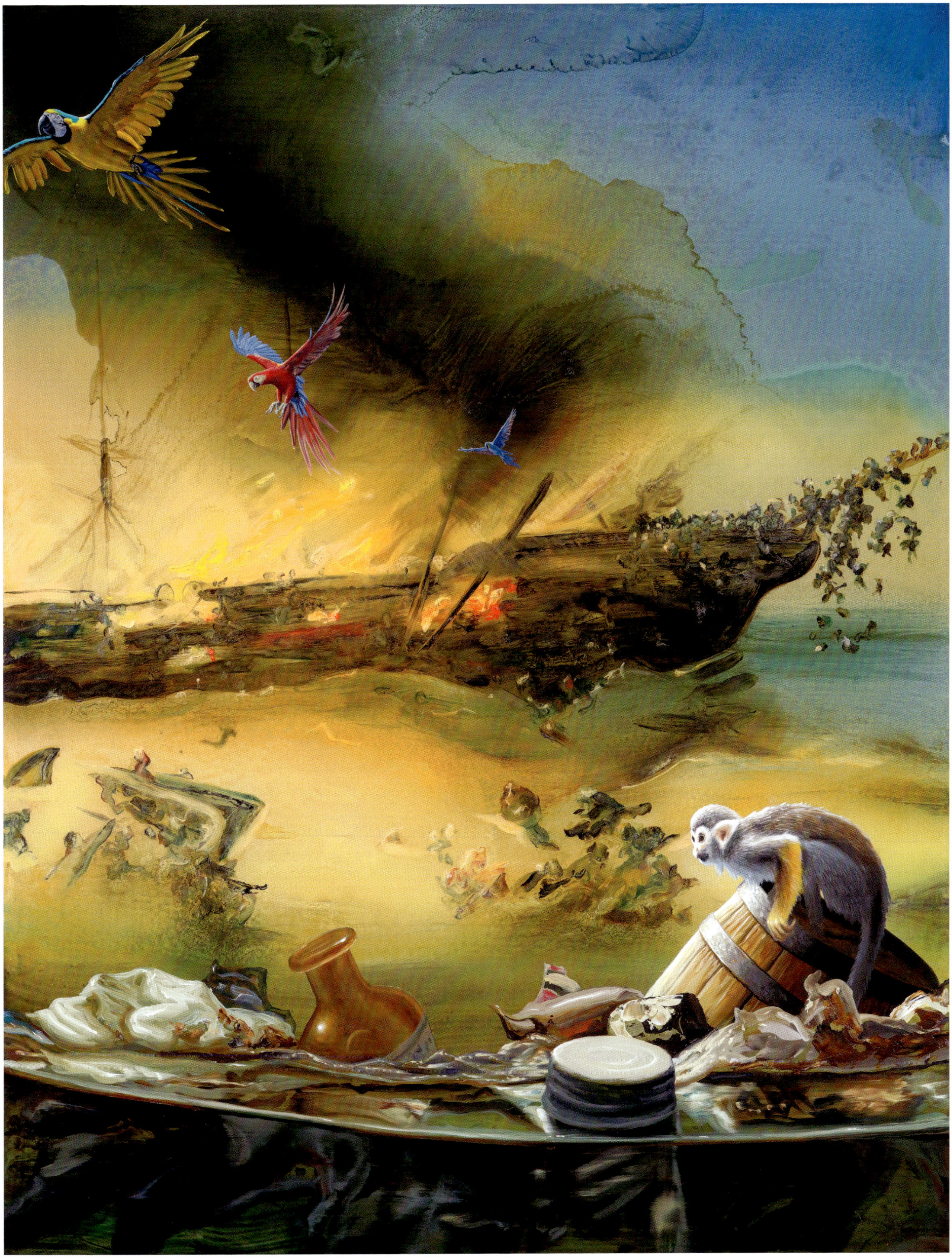

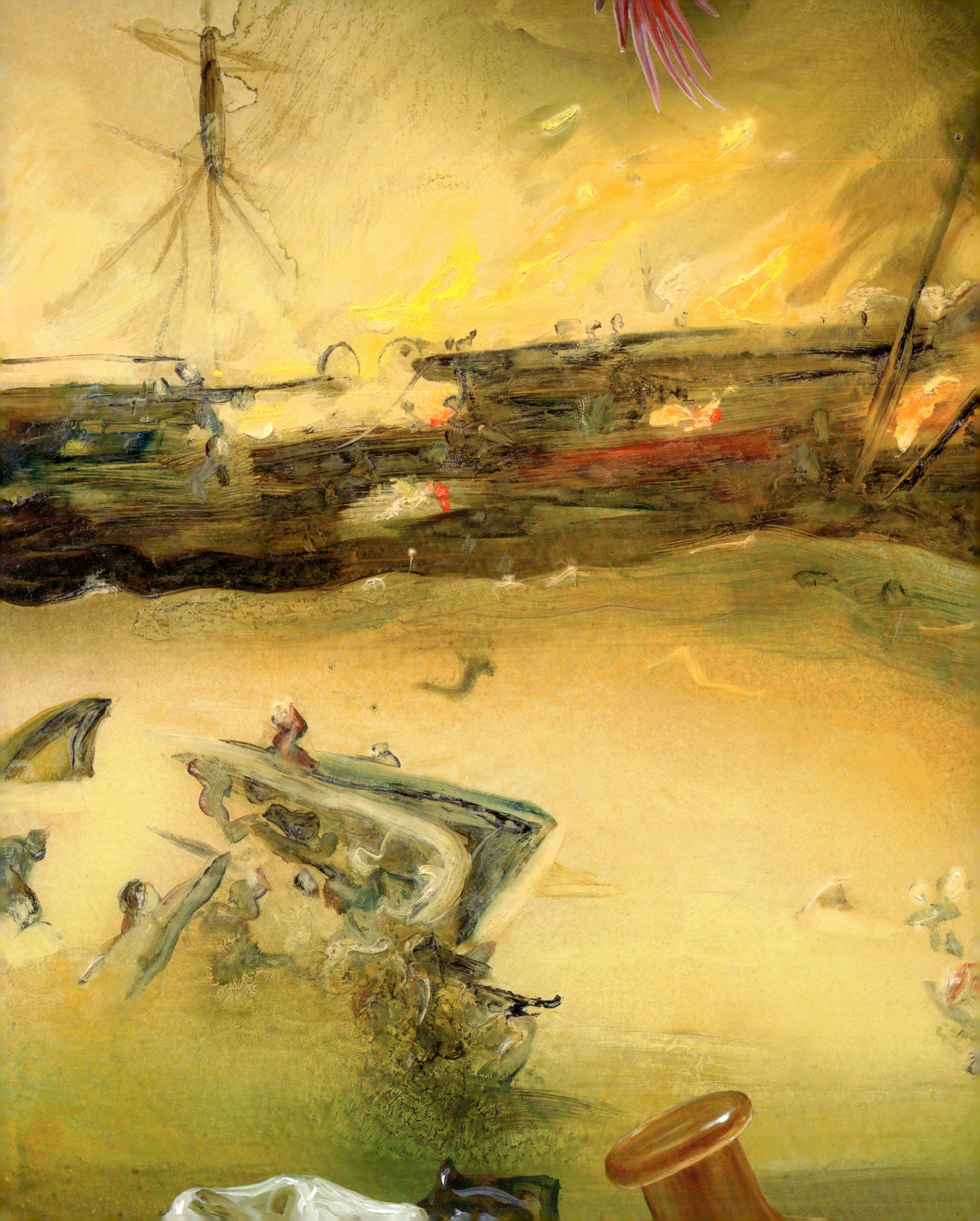

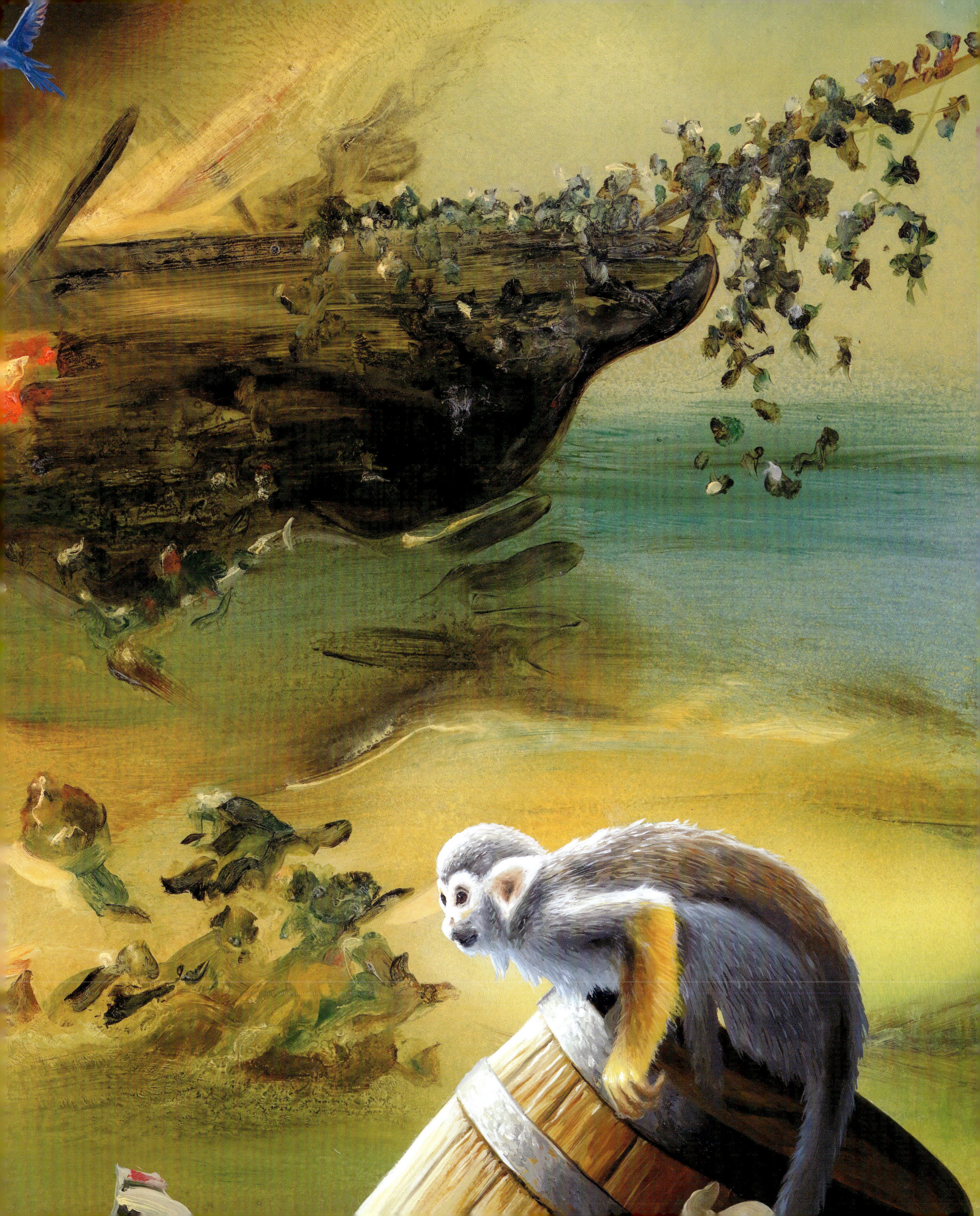

GLIDERS, 2017, WATERCOLOR, INK AND ACRYLIC ON PAPER, 24 X 18 IN.

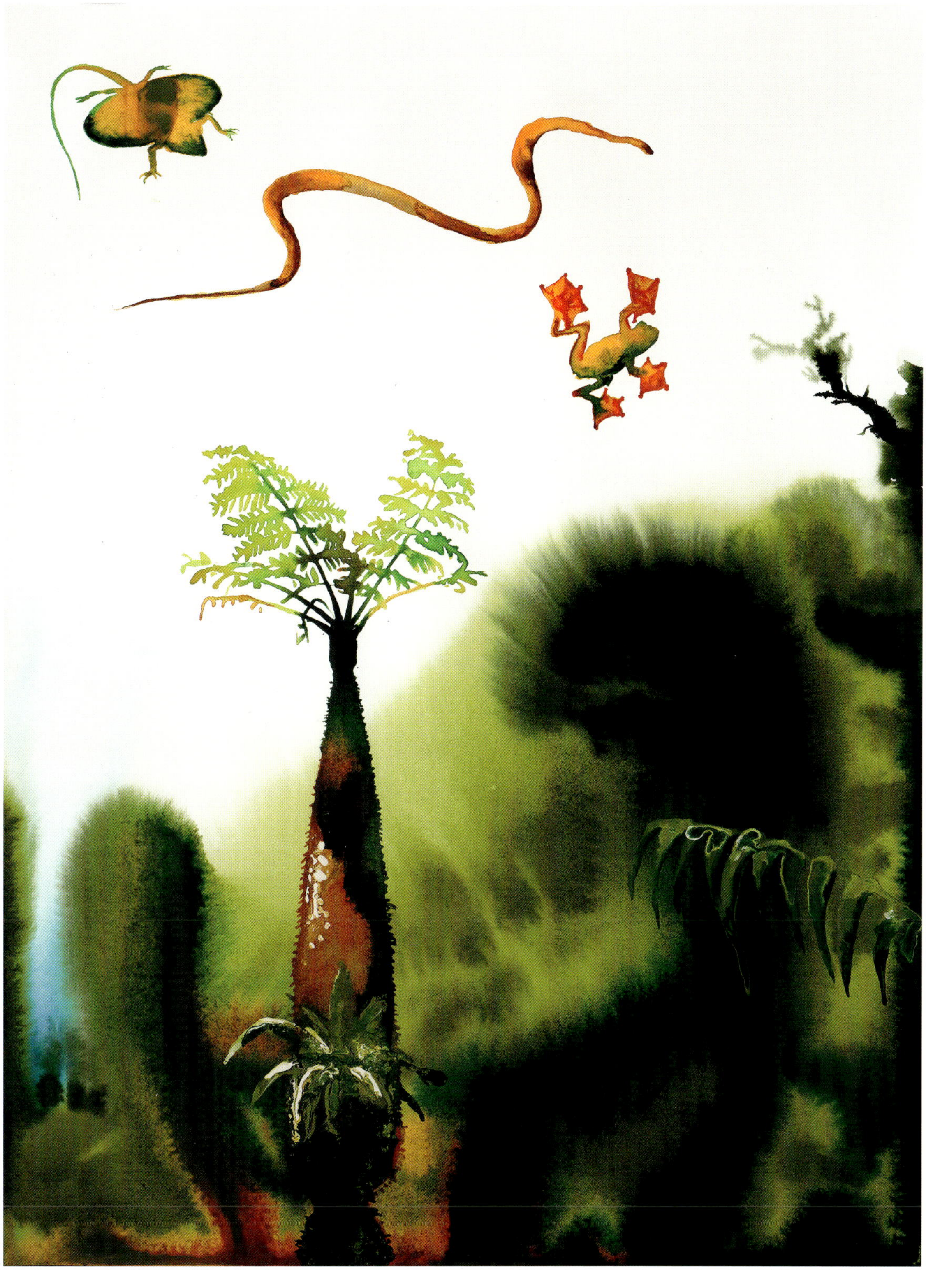

RAIN FOREST VISTA, 2017, WATERCOLOR AND INK ON PAPER, 18 X 24 IN.

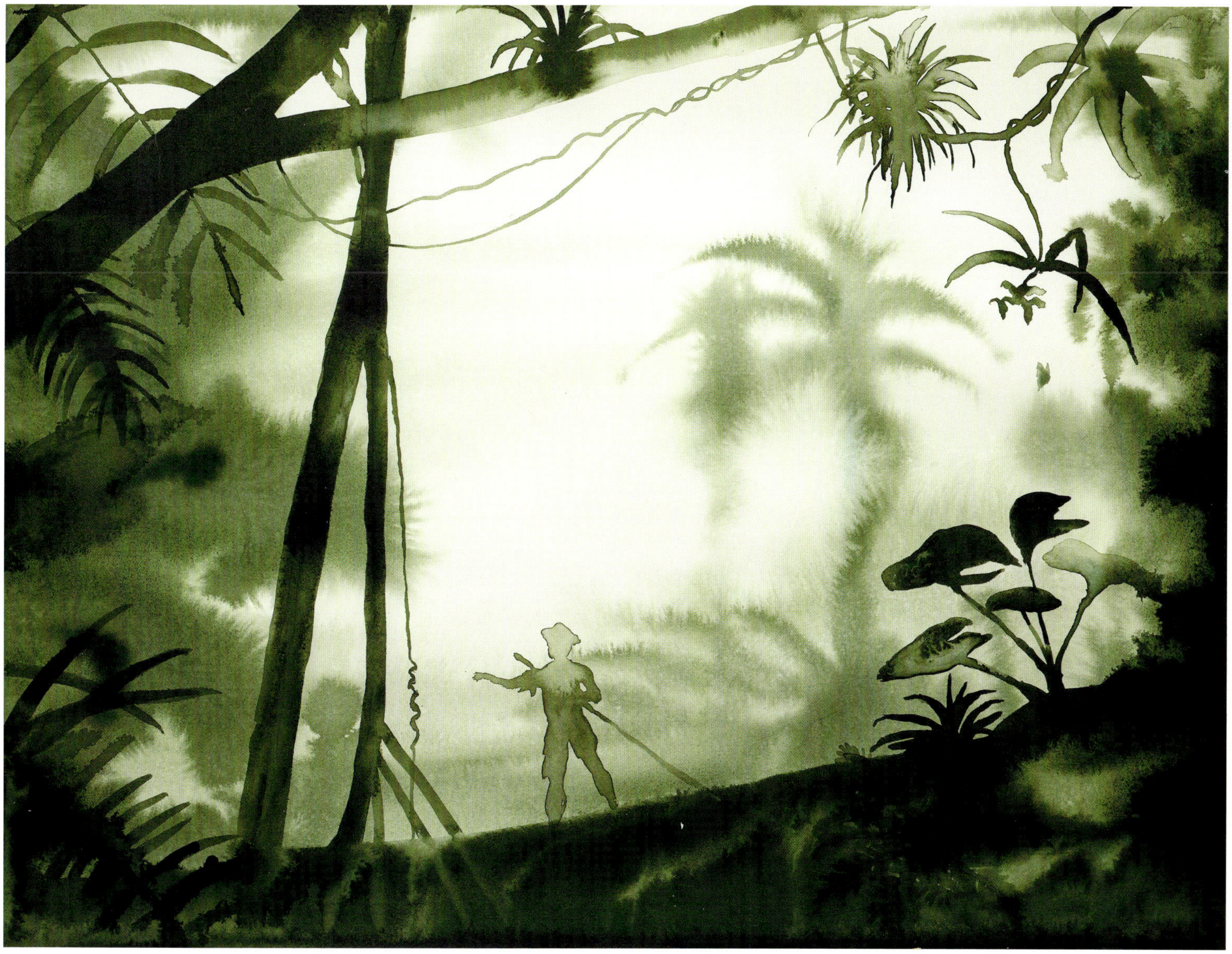

THE FLOODED FOREST, 2018, WATERCOLOR, INK AND ACRYLIC ON PAPER, 24 X 18 IN.

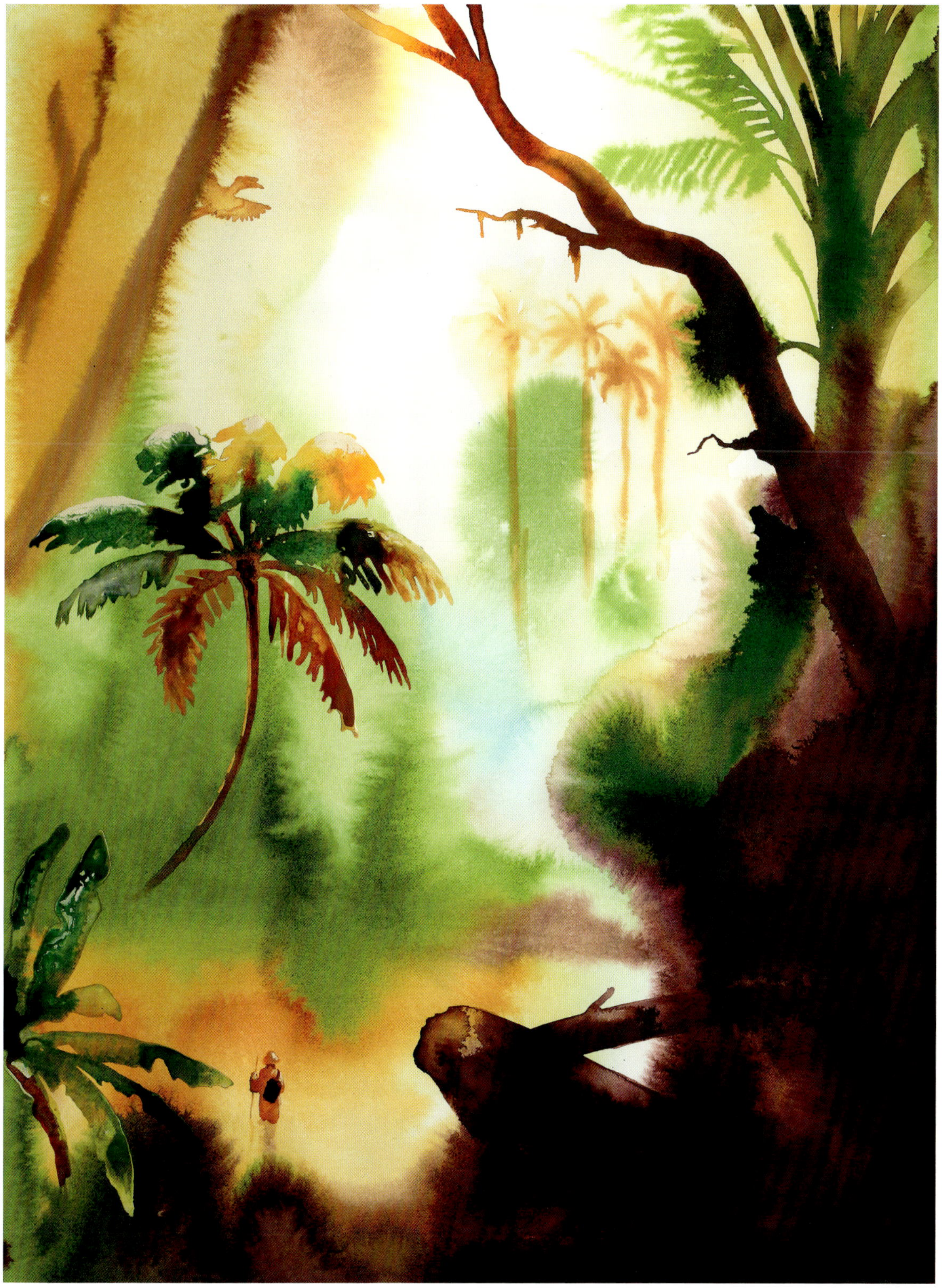

INVASION.

18 months after returning to London, Alfred Russel Wallace set off on his greatest expedition, going east this time to the Malay Archipelago (modern-day Malaysia, Indonesia, and New Guinea), a journey which was to last from 1854 to 1862. As before, Wallace traveled independently, financing his trip with the sales of specimens, enduring countless tropical nuisances, not least those on six legs. During a stay on the island of Wanumbai, a particularly aggressive type of ant invaded Wallace's hut and took dozens of specimens; a few enterprising if misguided workers even carried off some of the specimens' labels. A preview, perhaps, of the ravages of time, which scatters and consumes everything—bodies and names, lives and reputations—equally.

SPECIMEN LABELS, 2017, WATERCOLOR, INK AND ACRYLIC ON PAPER, 18 X 24 IN.

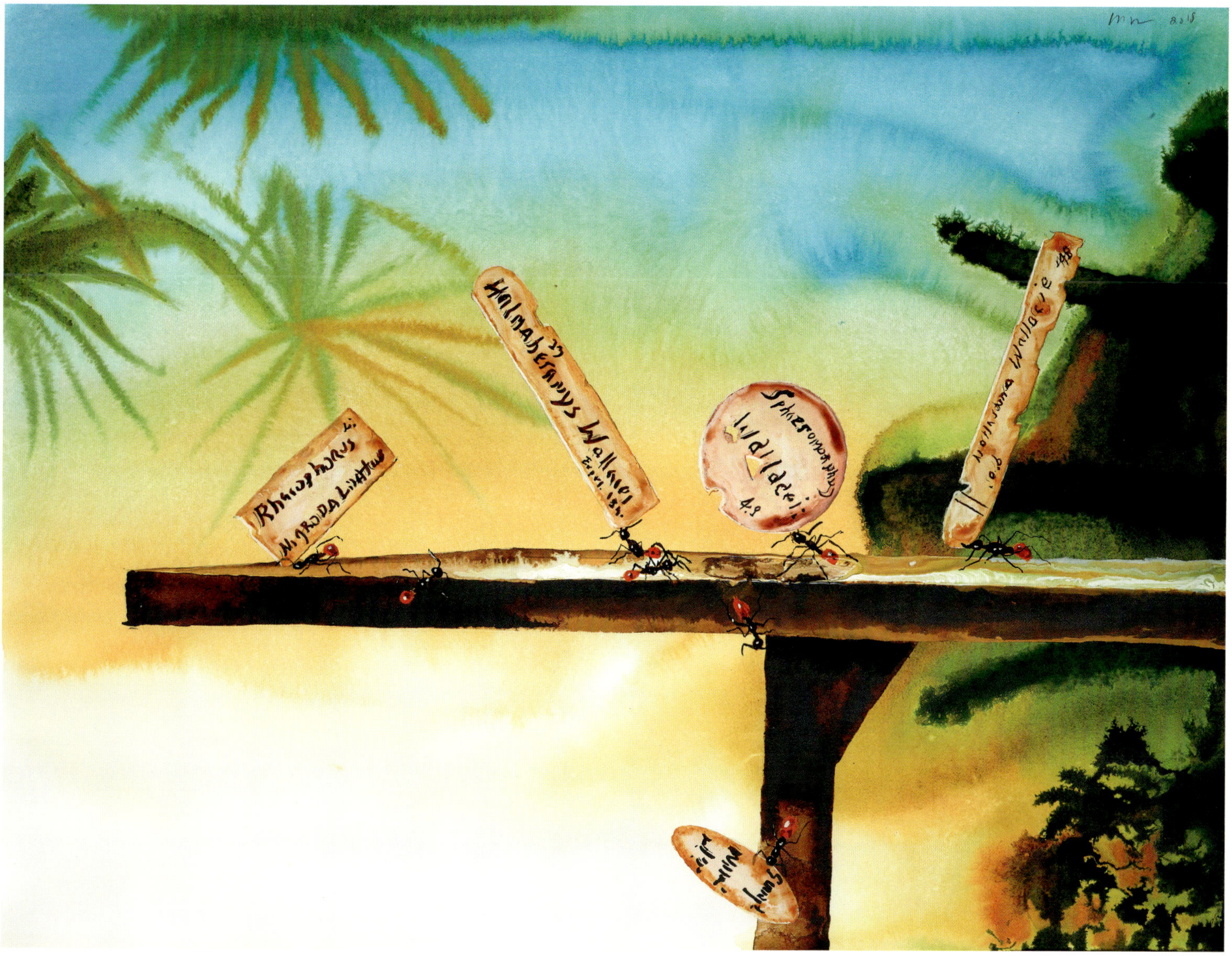

FOREST DRAGON, 2018, WATERCOLOR, INK AND ACRYLIC ON PAPER, 24 X 18 IN.

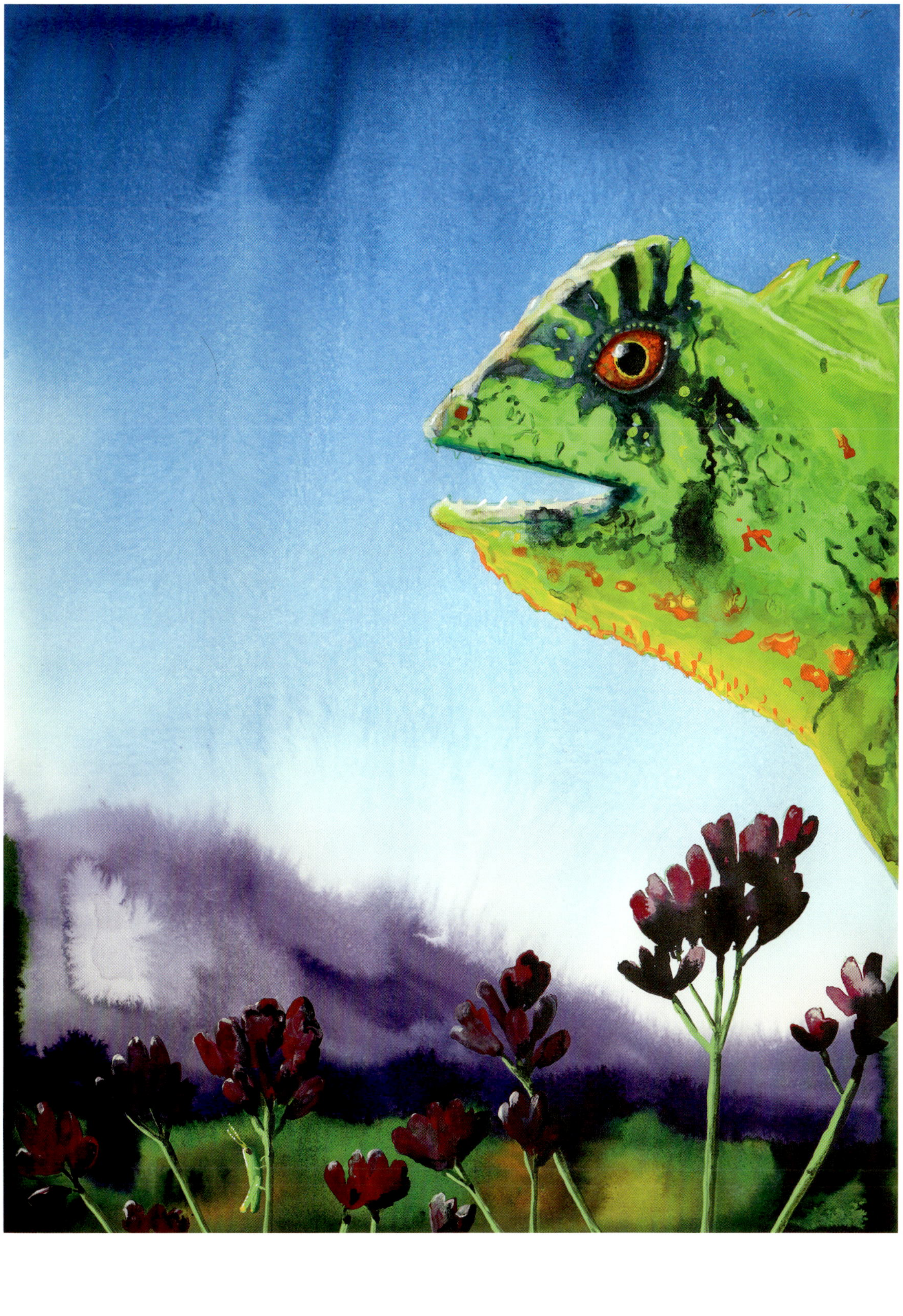

NAPENTHES, 2017, OIL AND ACRYLIC ON WOOD, 56 X 44 IN.

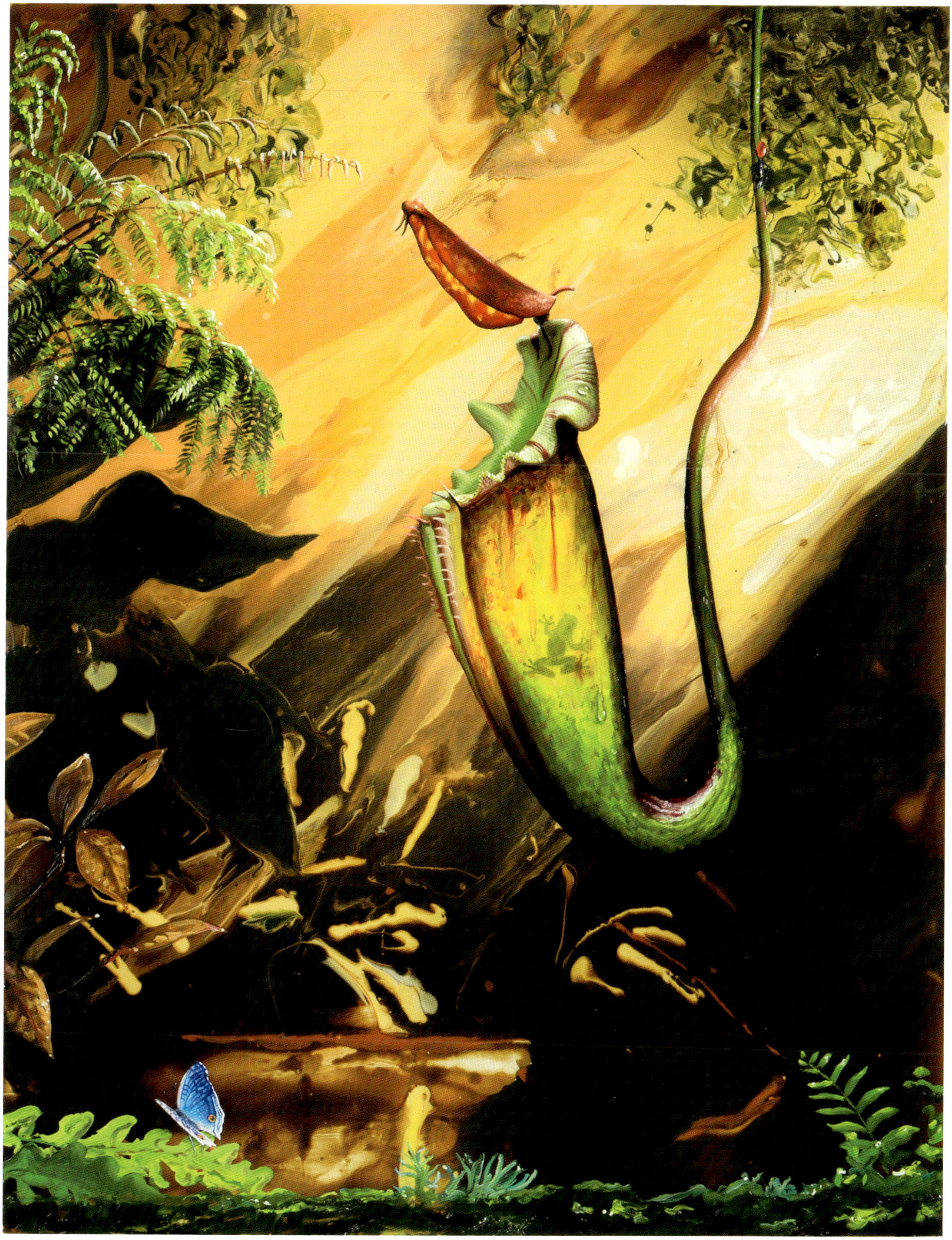

THE INTERVIEW, 2018, WATERCOLOR AND INK ON PAPER, 18 X 24 IN.

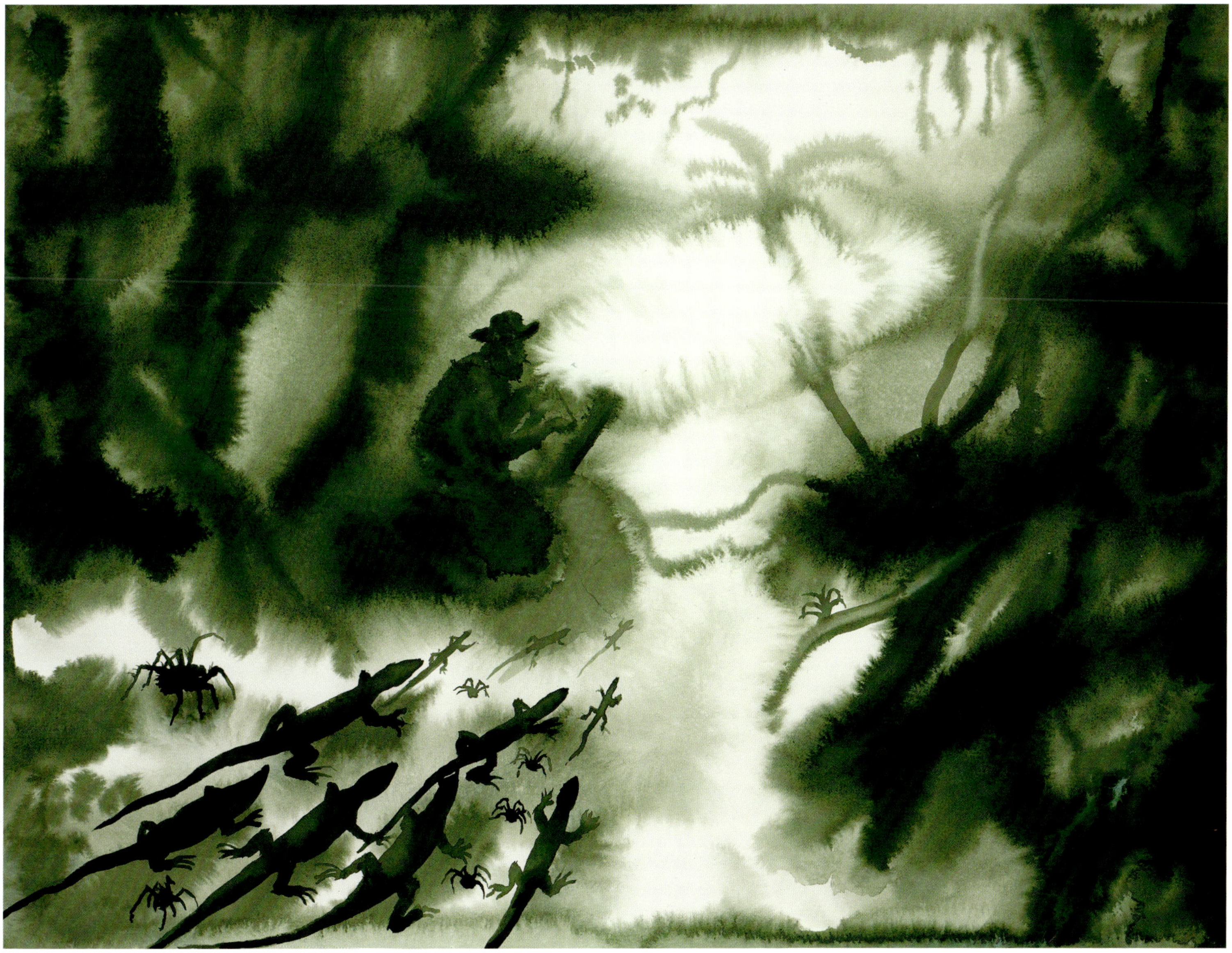

BUTTERFLY COLLECTOR, 2018, WATERCOLOR, INK AND ACRYLIC ON PAPER, 24 X 18 IN.

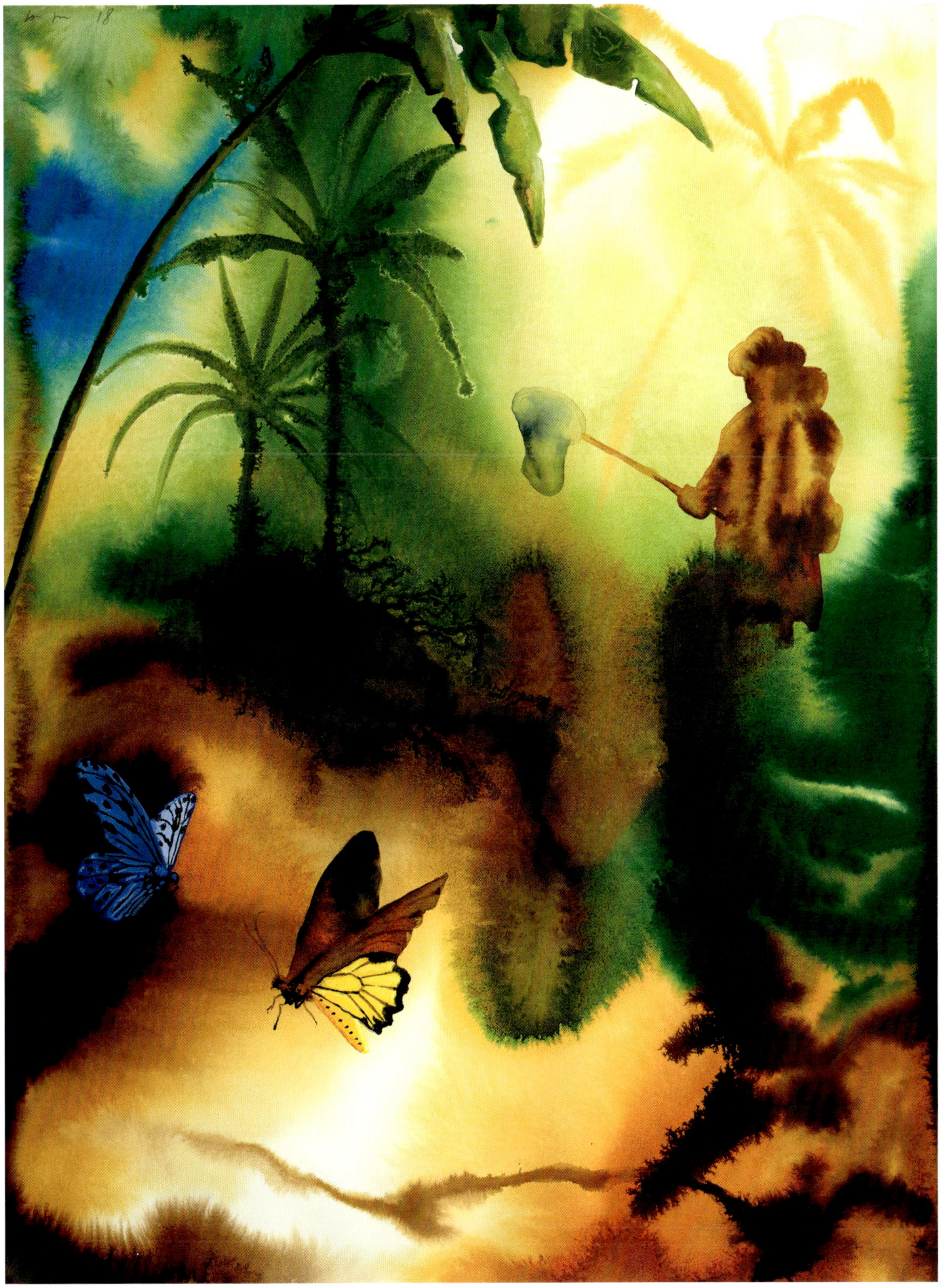

RHINOCEROS HORNBILL, 2017, WATERCOLOR, INK AND ACRYLIC ON PAPER, 24 X 18 IN.

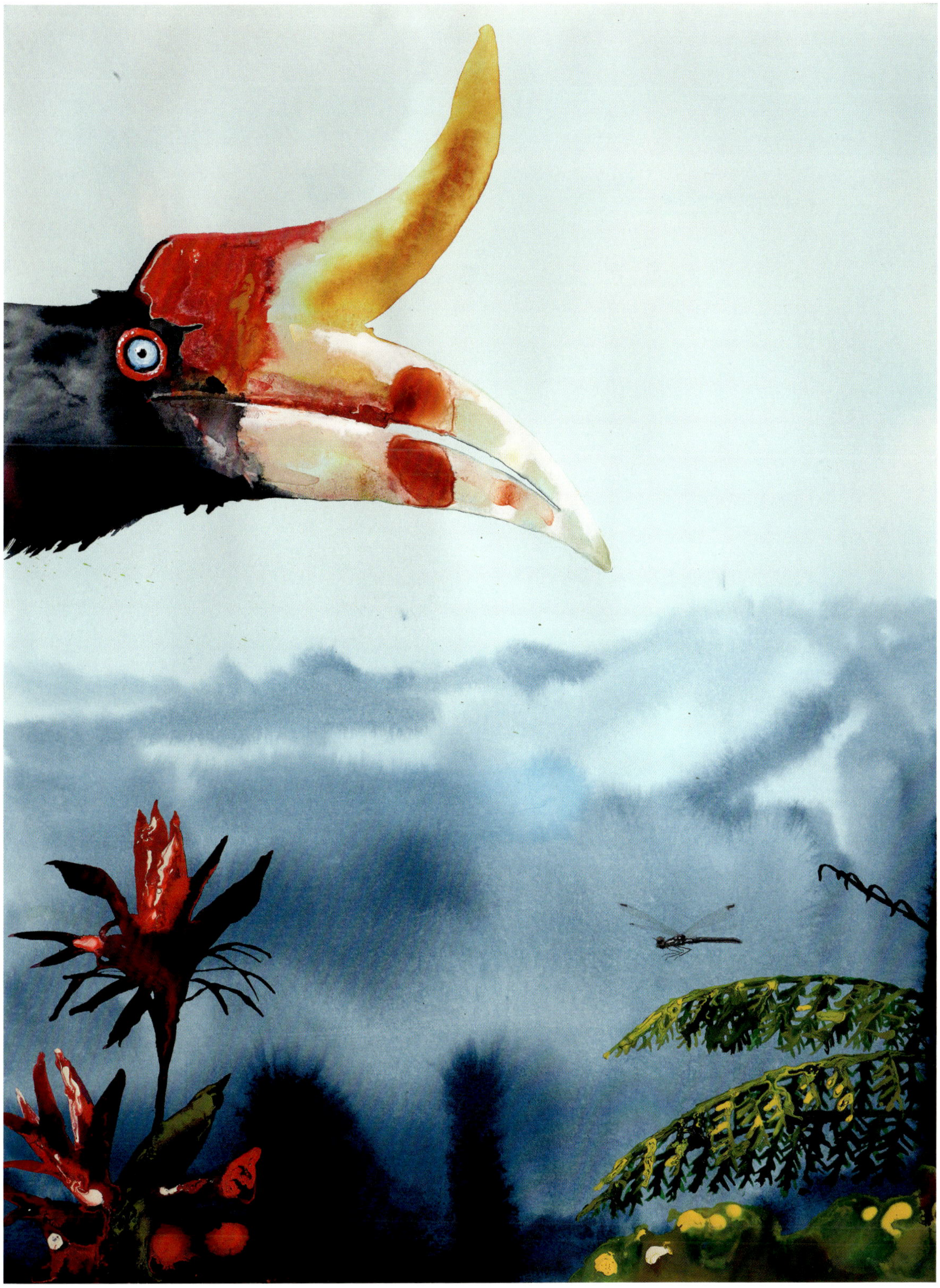

AZURE KINGFISHER, 2017, OIL AND ACRYLIC ON WOOD, 56 X 44 IN.

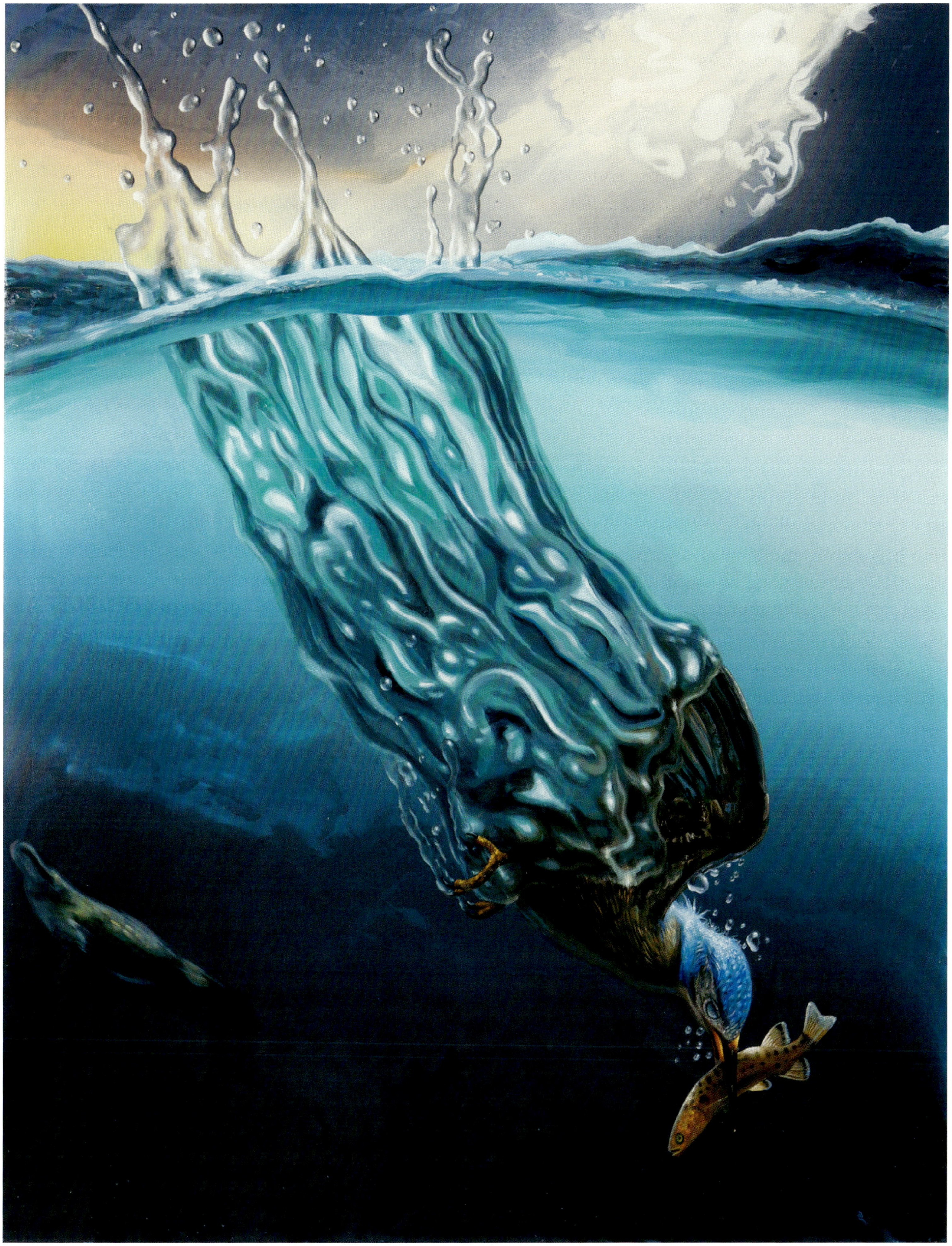

CONVERGENCE.

The elusive nature of fame is bound up with Alfred Russel Wallace's journey. Wallace had formulated one of the most influential ideas in the history of science—natural selection as the engine of evolution—independently from Darwin; but it was Darwin who made it to the finish line with his book, *On The Origin of Species*, which was largely written under the impetus of Wallace's parallel discovery. Two remarkable, almost identical theories—it's like the chance encounter, on a tree, between two different species of birds-of-paradise, both relatives of the common crow who have, independently of one another, evolved a similar set of extravagant displays to get attention from the opposite sex. Among many other insects and animals, Wallace has a bird-of-paradise which he first discovered, Wallace's Standardwing, named after him. But Wallace's rival got the far bigger prize: the -ism at the end of Darwin's name that signifies an entire scientific revolution, one that continues to this day.

A STRIKING COINCIDENCE, 2018, OIL AND ACRYLIC ON WOOD, 18 X 24 IN.

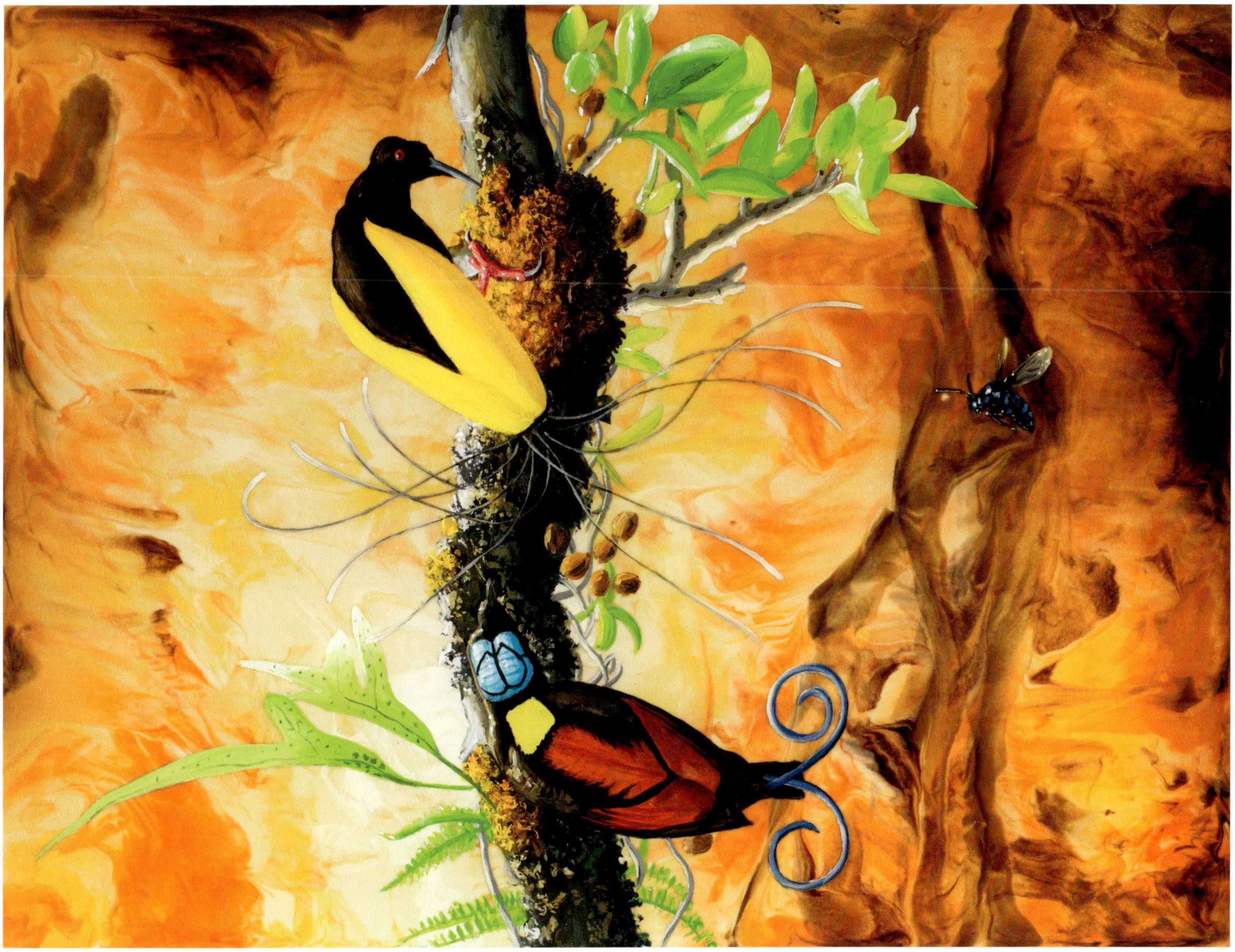

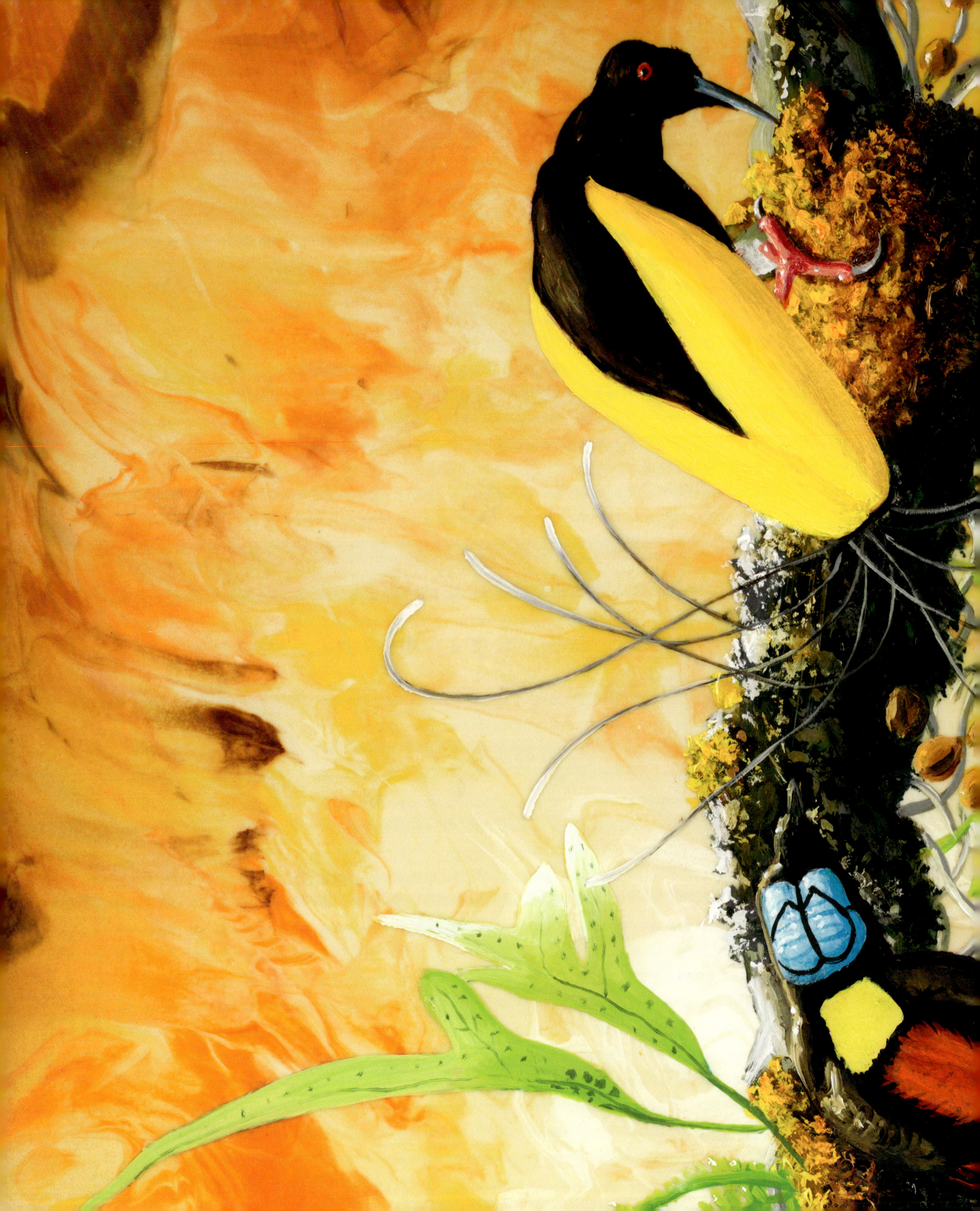

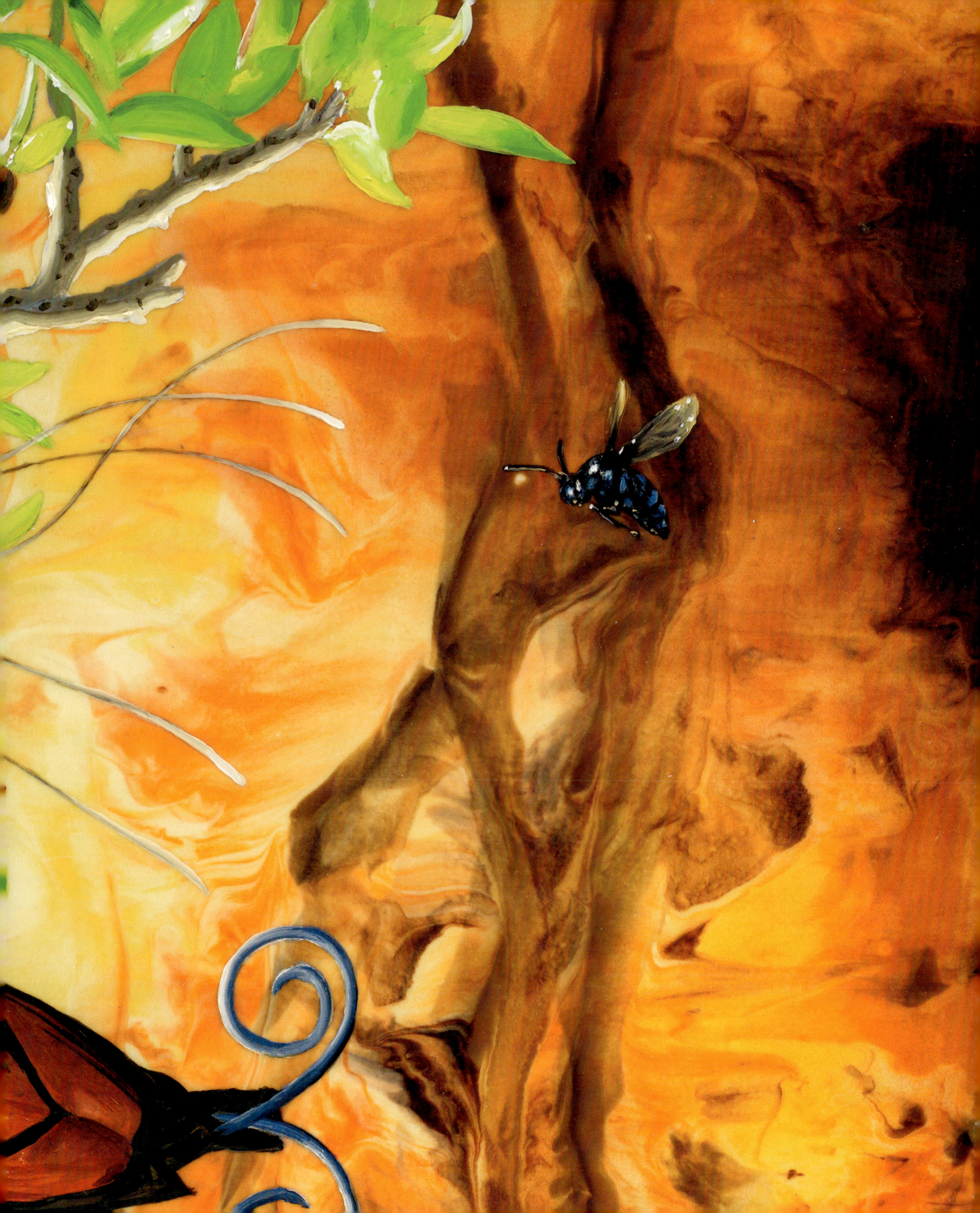

LOSS OF FAITH, 2018, WATERCOLOR, INK AND ACRYLIC ON PAPER, 18 X 24 IN.

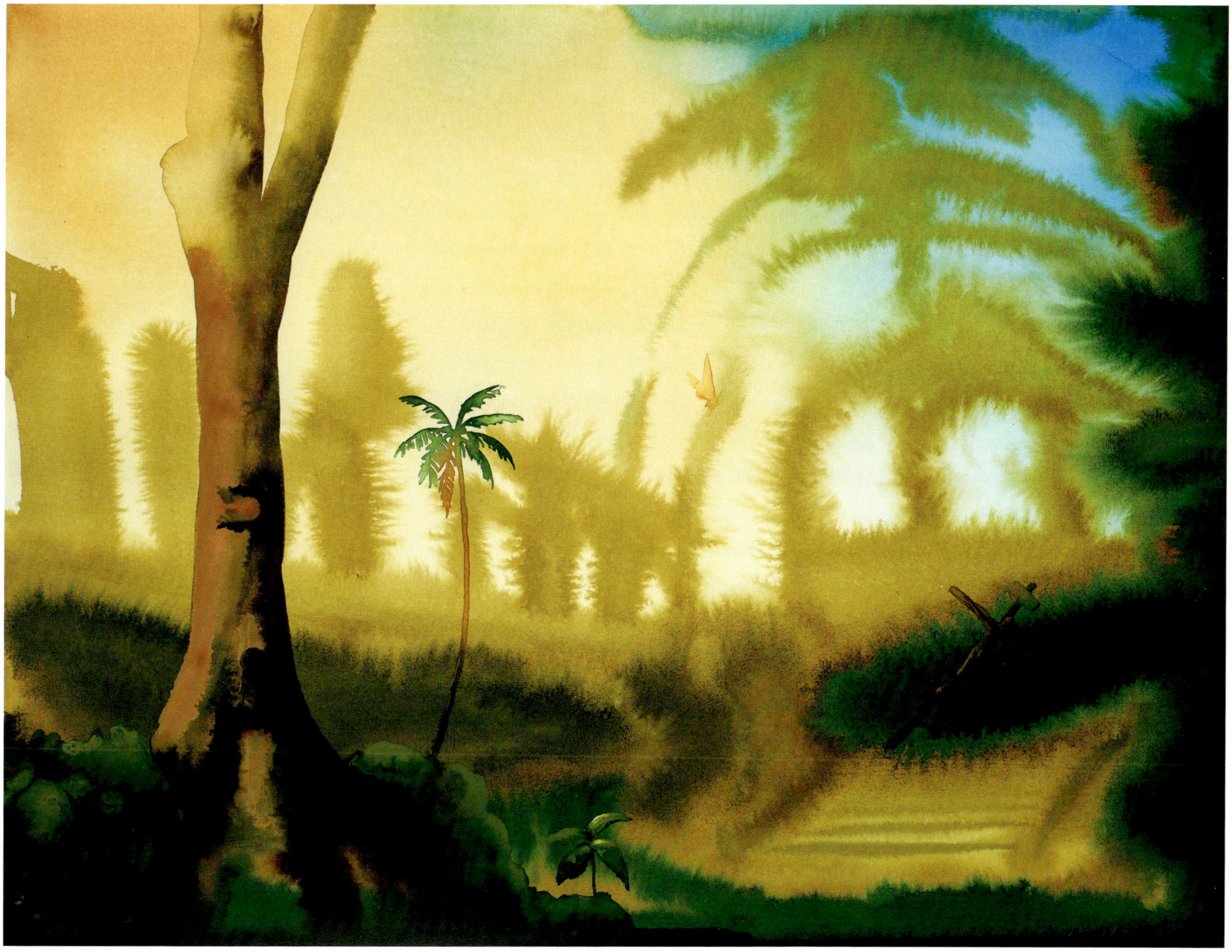

COLLECTING BIRDS-OF-PARADISE, 2018, WATERCOLOR, INK AND ACRYLIC ON PAPER, 24 X 18 IN.

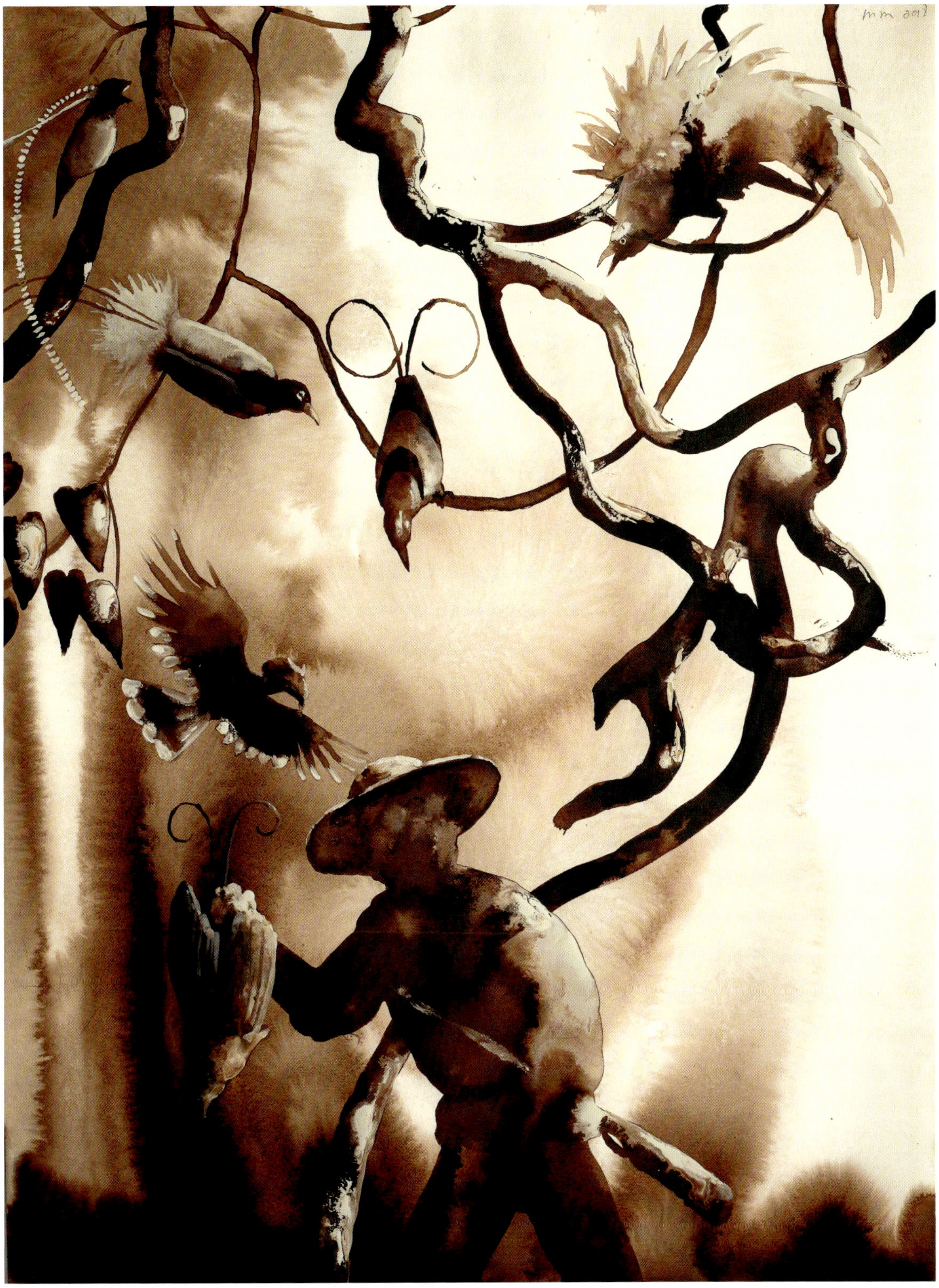

VISION.
(*The Hammock* and *Fever Dream*)

While Alfred Russel Wallace slept in his hammock one night, a mosquito flew in and, with one bite, changed the course of scientific history. It was during the resulting bout of yellow fever that Wallace, his head spinning with memories and ideas, came up with the idea of natural selection. Here, through Wallace's hallucinating eyes, we re-imagine the tree of life—the familiar diagram of the evolution of species—as a literal, living tree: a giant banyan with each species on its own branch. As the tree thrusts upward and ramifies, some animals manage to hang on, while others—Thylacine, or the Tasmanian tiger, for example—fall, extinct, to the ground. The tree is also a map, alluding to Wallace's other great discovery, as the trunk divides the animals of Asia on one side from the animals of Australasia on the other.

THE HAMMOCK, 2018, WATERCOLOR, INK AND ACRYLIC ON PAPER, 18 X 24 IN.

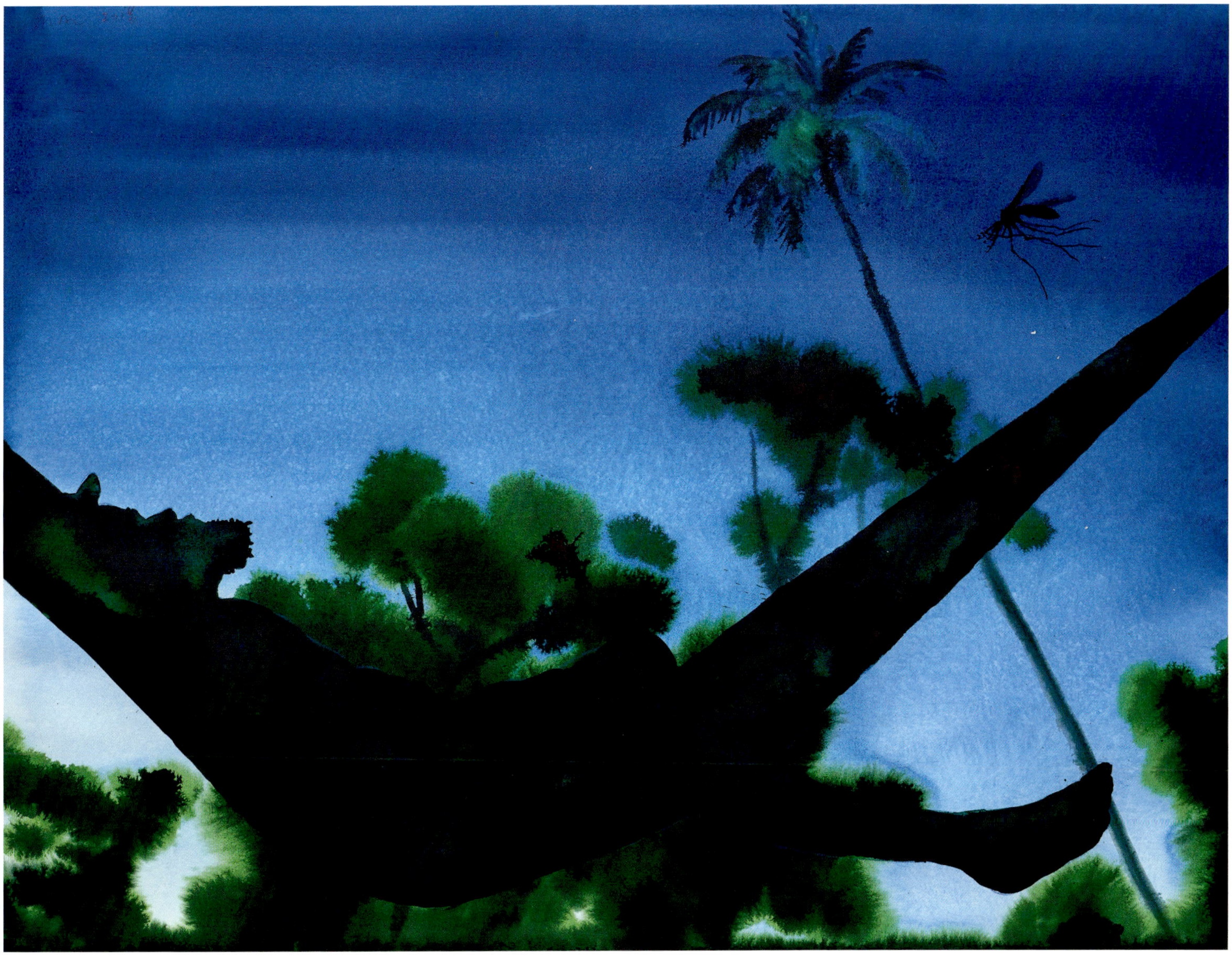

FEVER DREAM, 2018, OIL ON WOOD, 80 X 68 IN.

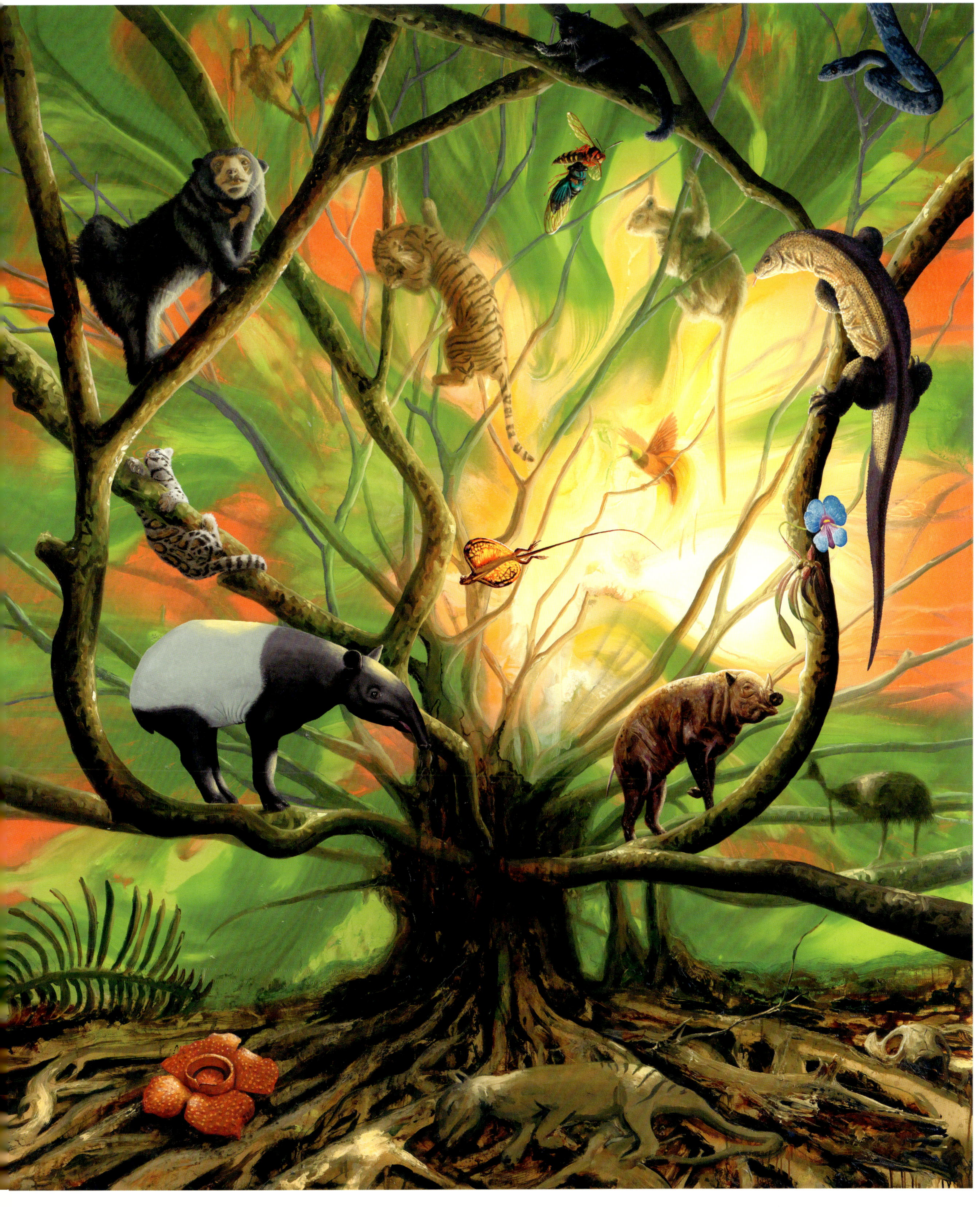

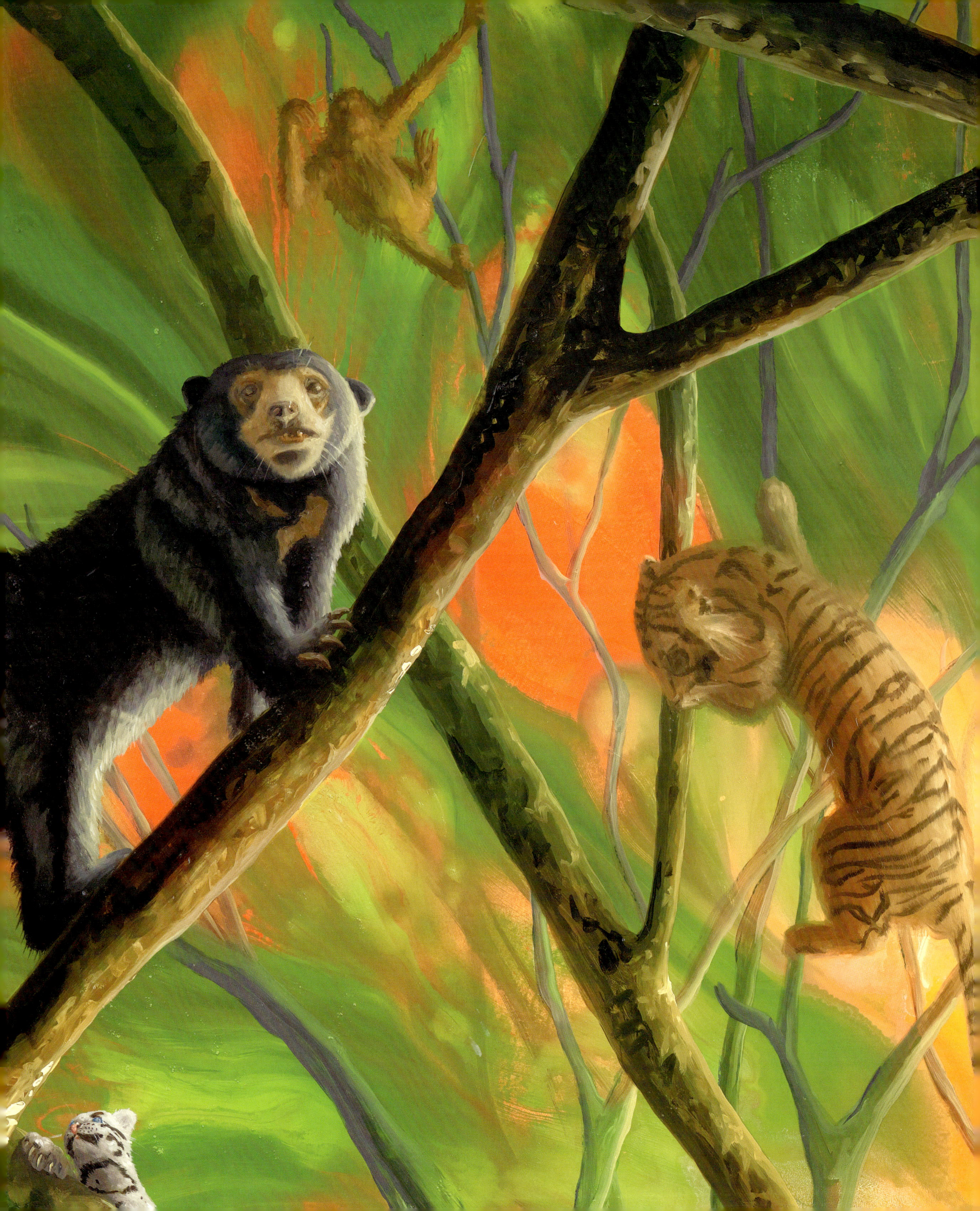

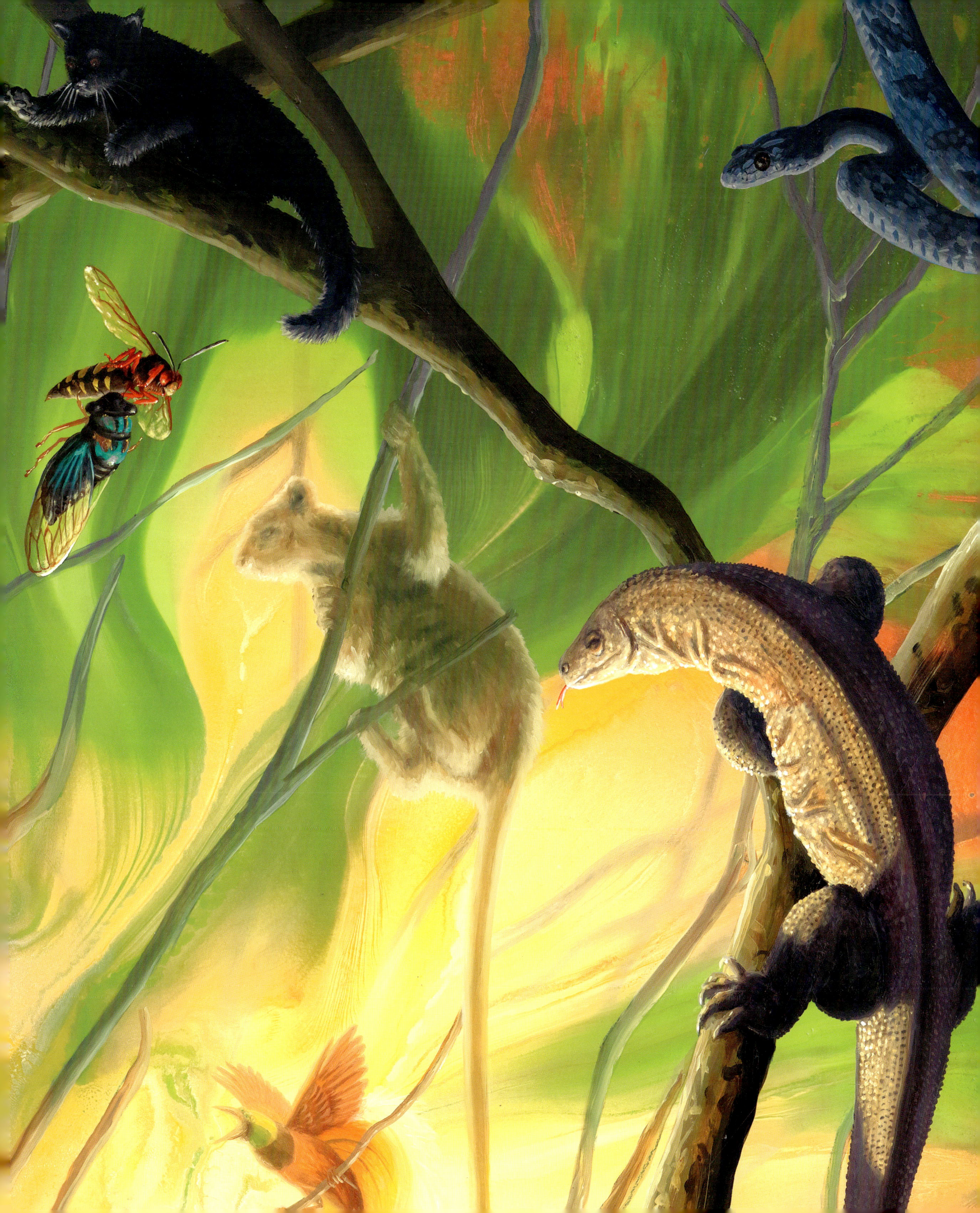

THE LINE.

Only on a painted map (or perhaps in a badly-run zoo) could the two most iconic Indonesian animals—the orangutan and the Komodo dragon—be seen duking it out. In reality, the two are separated not only by water and islands, but more fundamentally, by the invisible line between Asian fauna and the fauna of Australasia. Alfred Russel Wallace discovered this division when he crossed the narrow strait between the islands of Bali and Lombok, and found a completely different assortment of birds and mammals—including parrots and marsupials—on the other side of the narrow strait. The Wallace Line (named in his honor) was part of a new scientific discipline that Wallace largely established: biogeography, or the study of the geographical distribution of species. It's also a fitting metaphor for Wallace's career, over the course of which he crossed so many boundaries—of class, society, empire, science, spirituality and politics.

WALLACE'S LINE, 2017, OIL ON DIBOND, 18 X 24 IN.

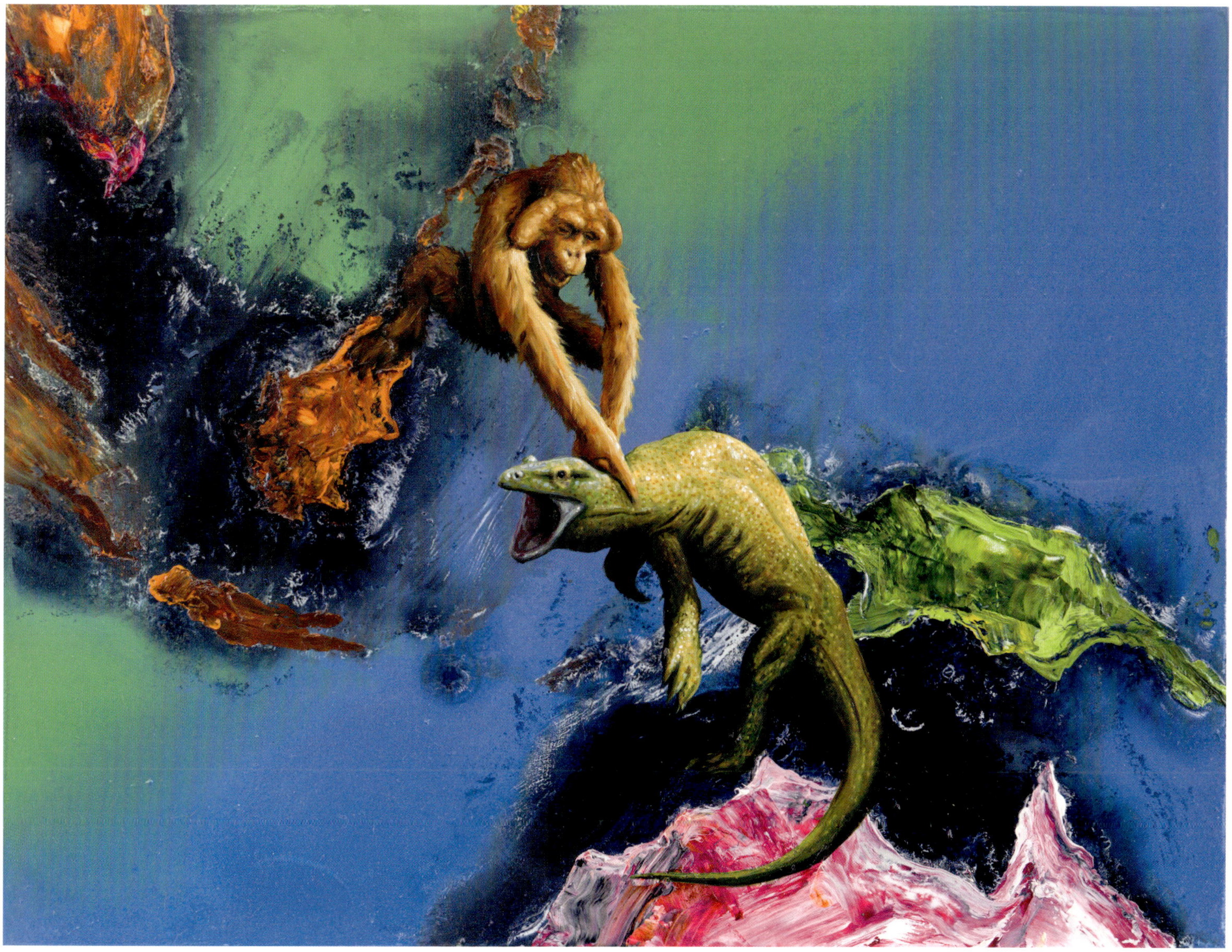

WALLACE'S VISION, 2017, OIL AND ACRYLIC ON WOOD, 24 X 36 IN.

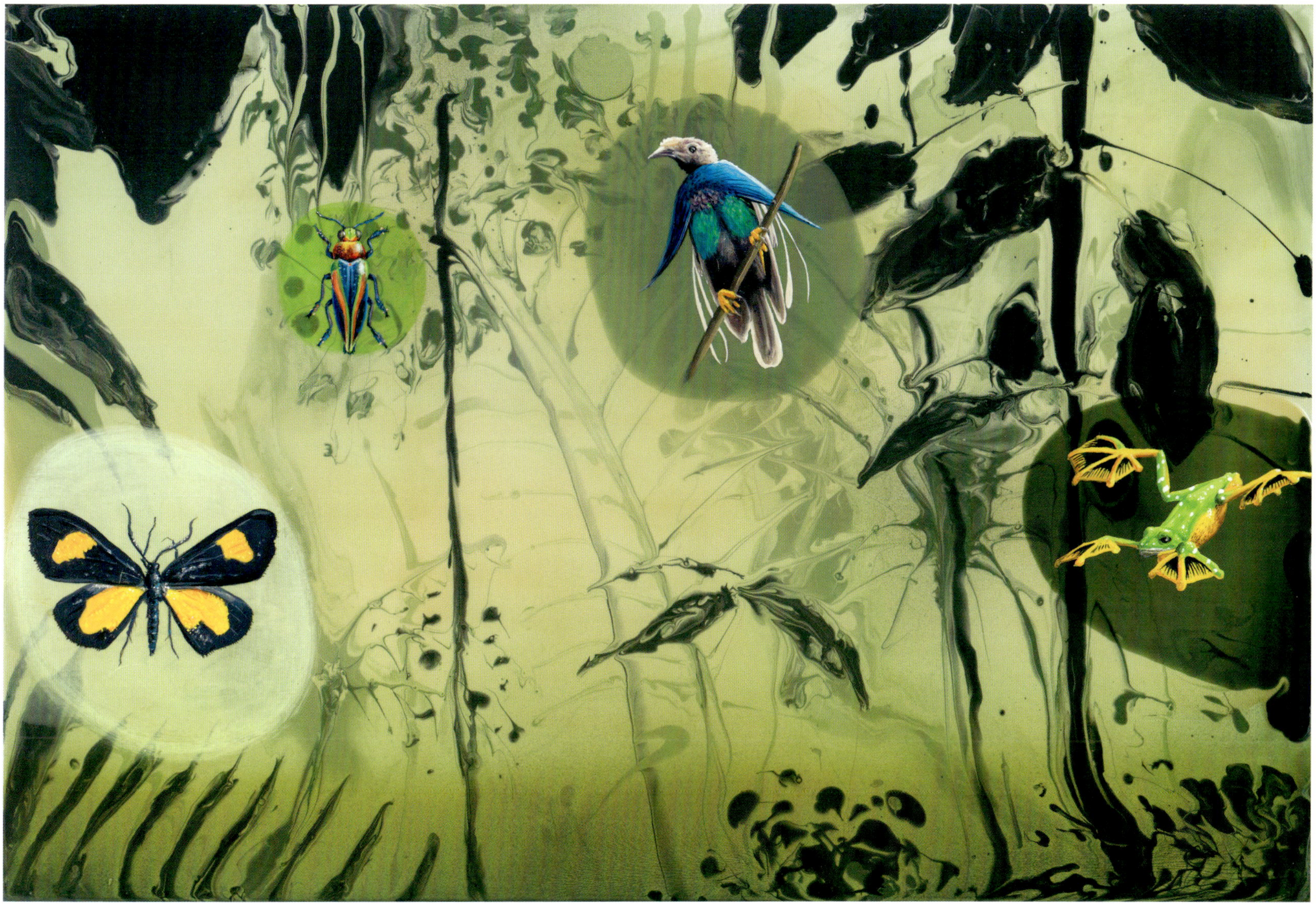

CONCRETE JUNGLE IN LONDON, 2018, OIL ON DIBOND, 18 X 24 IN.

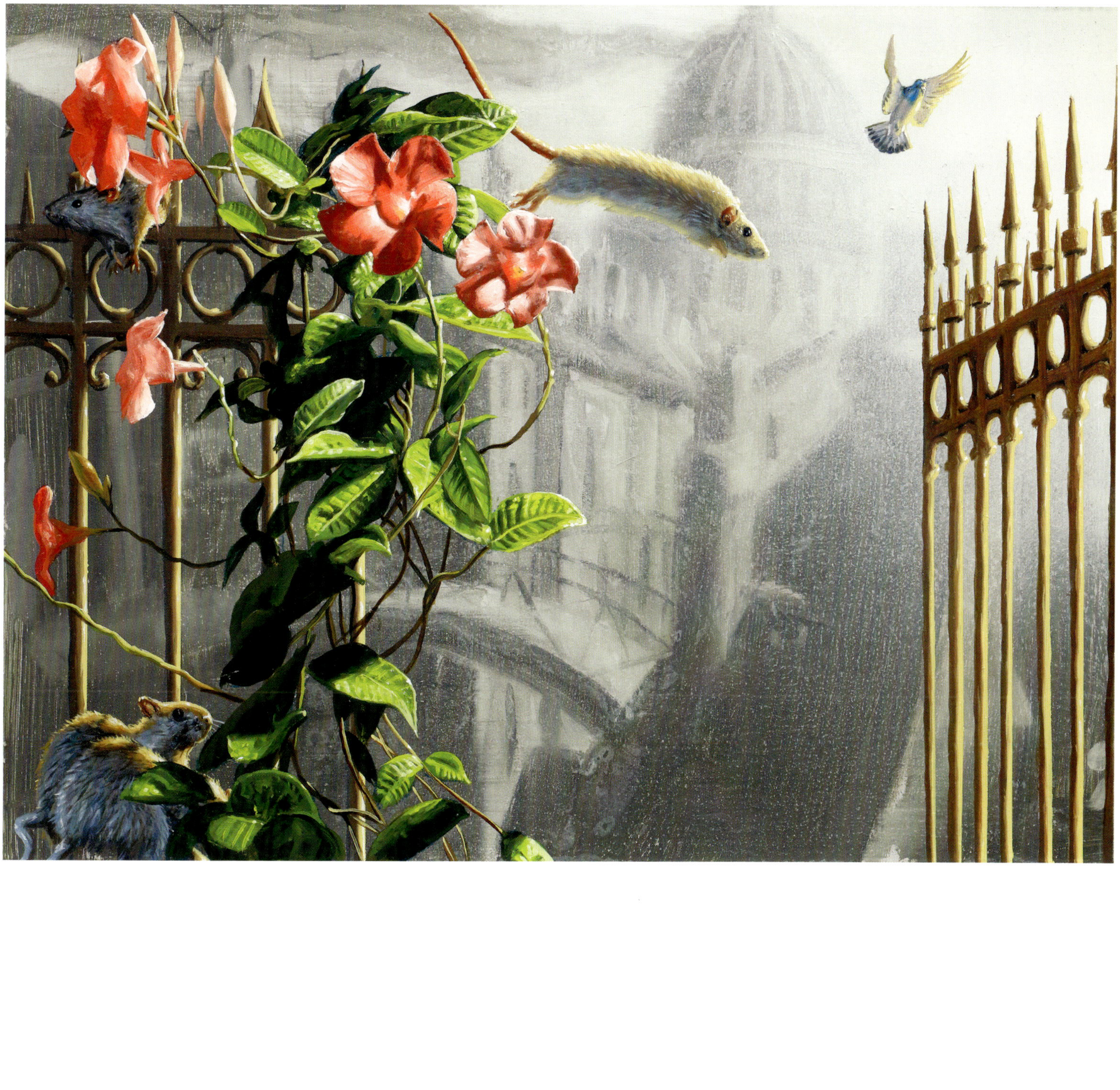

LOVE.

Courtship and reproduction are cornerstones of evolutionary biology. Humans call it "love," and, in the hothouse of society and family, cultivate it like a flower. As Alfred Russel Wallace sits with his future wife Annie in London's Kew Gardens, their wooing is haloed by a circle of pollen-bearing insects, birds and fruit bats—symbols of fertility to bless the new couple. The startled gaze of the slow loris peering over the Victoria water lily perhaps echoes our own surprise, that Wallace—so peripatetic and also rather awkward with women—should finally be settling down. Or maybe departing again on a very different journey, to the unknown interior of himself.

COURTSHIP BEHAVIOR, 2018, OIL ON DIBOND, 44 X 56 IN.

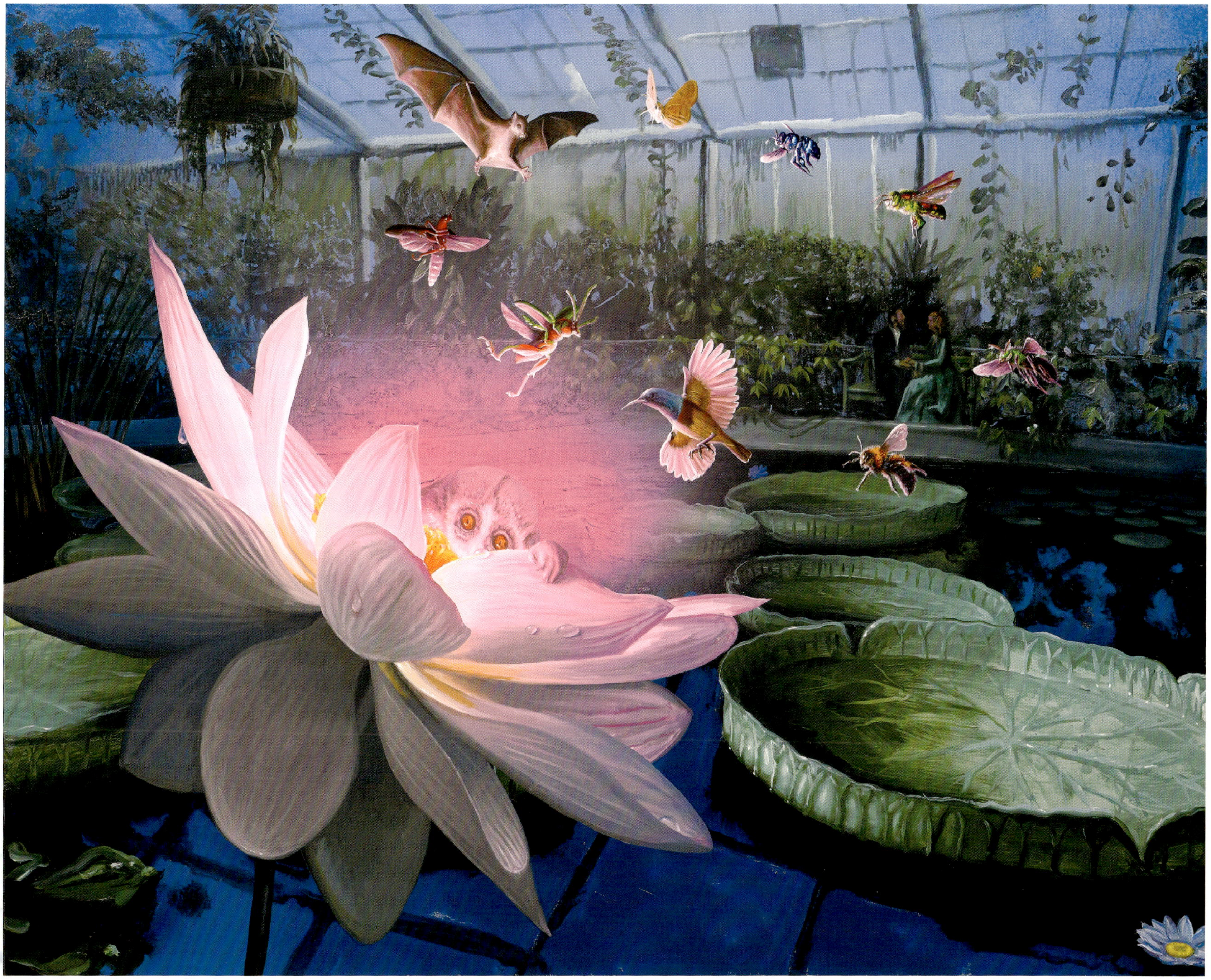

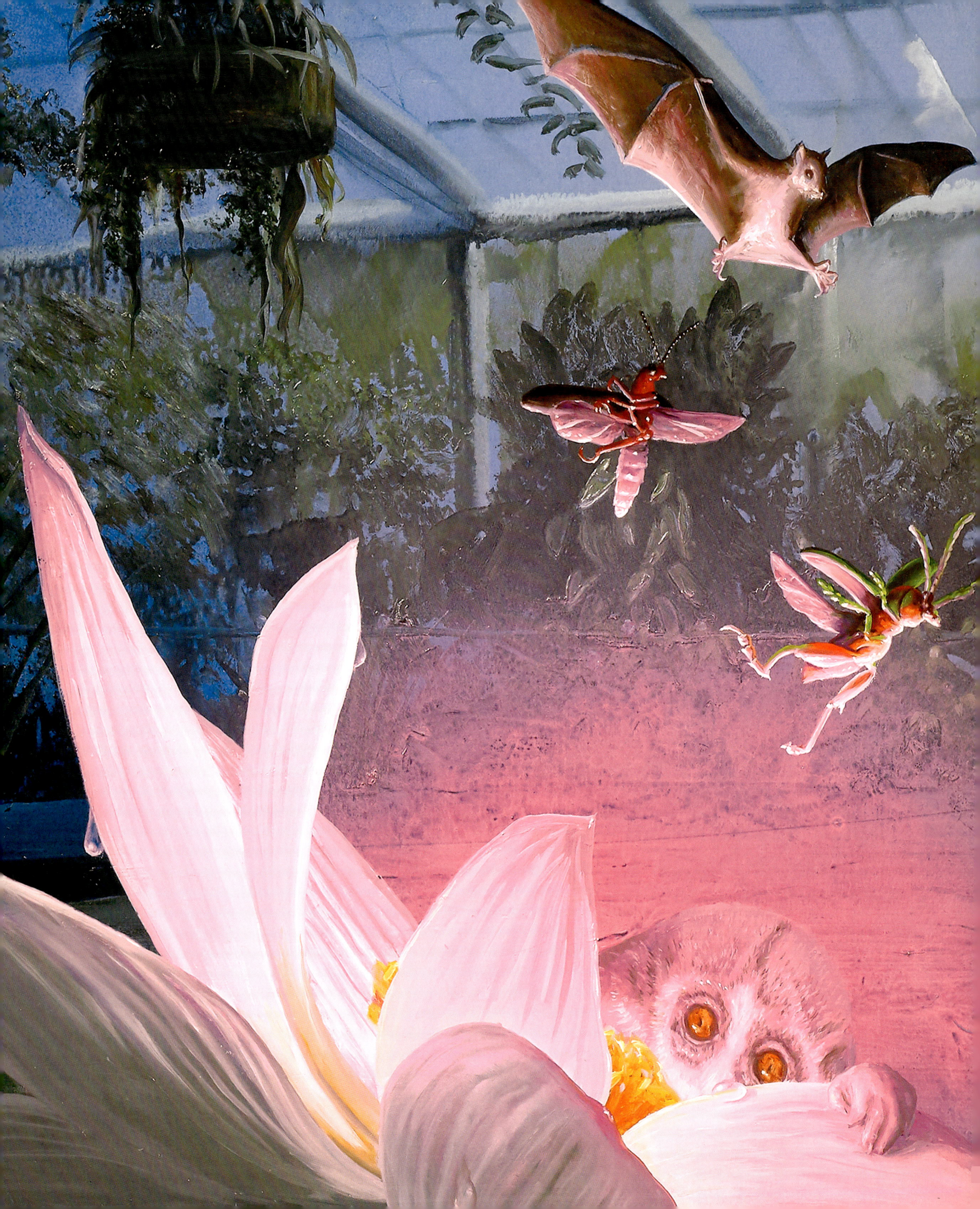

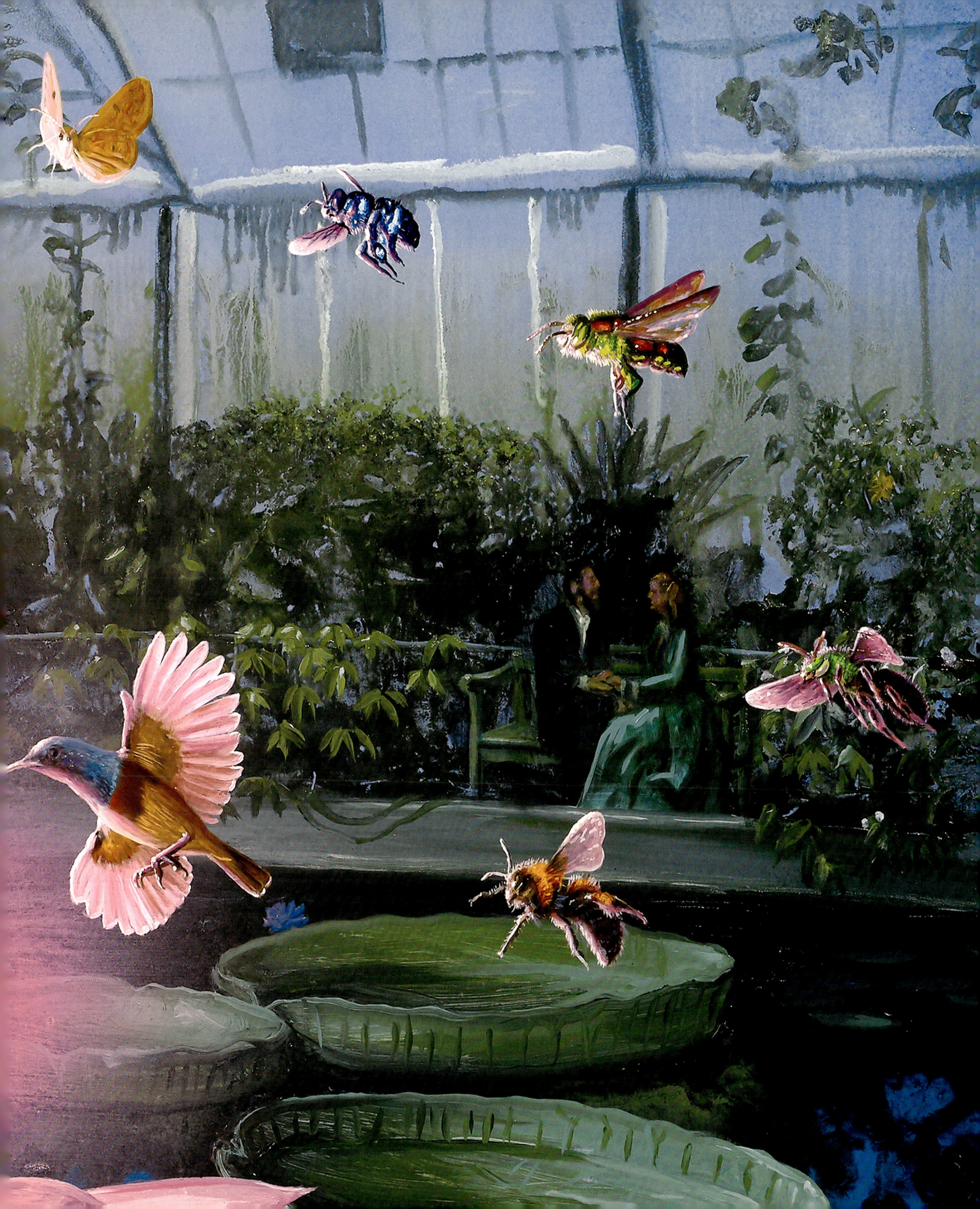

KEYS TO THE PAINTINGS.

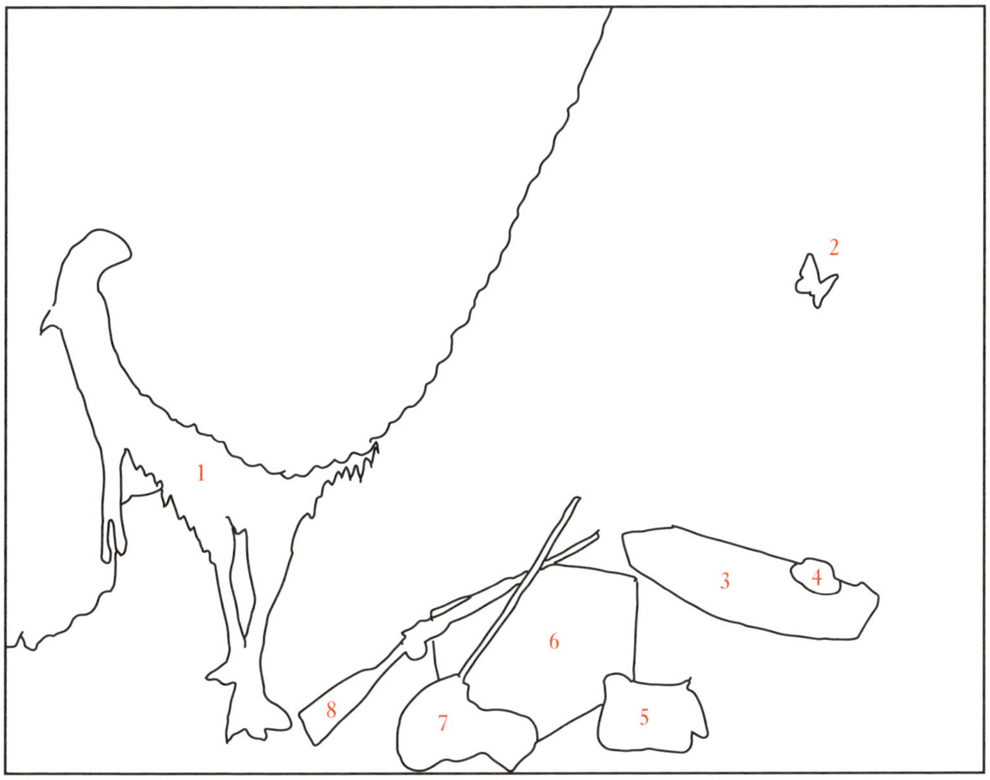

Departure, page 9.

1. Northern Cassowary *(Casuarius unappendiculatus)*
2. Orange Albatross *(Appias nero)*
3. Perahu Panjang Longboat
4. Stetson Panama Straw Fedora Hat
5. Leather Satchel
6. Specimen Campaign Trunk
7. Insect Collecting Net
8. Brunswick Rifle, Lacy & Co, London

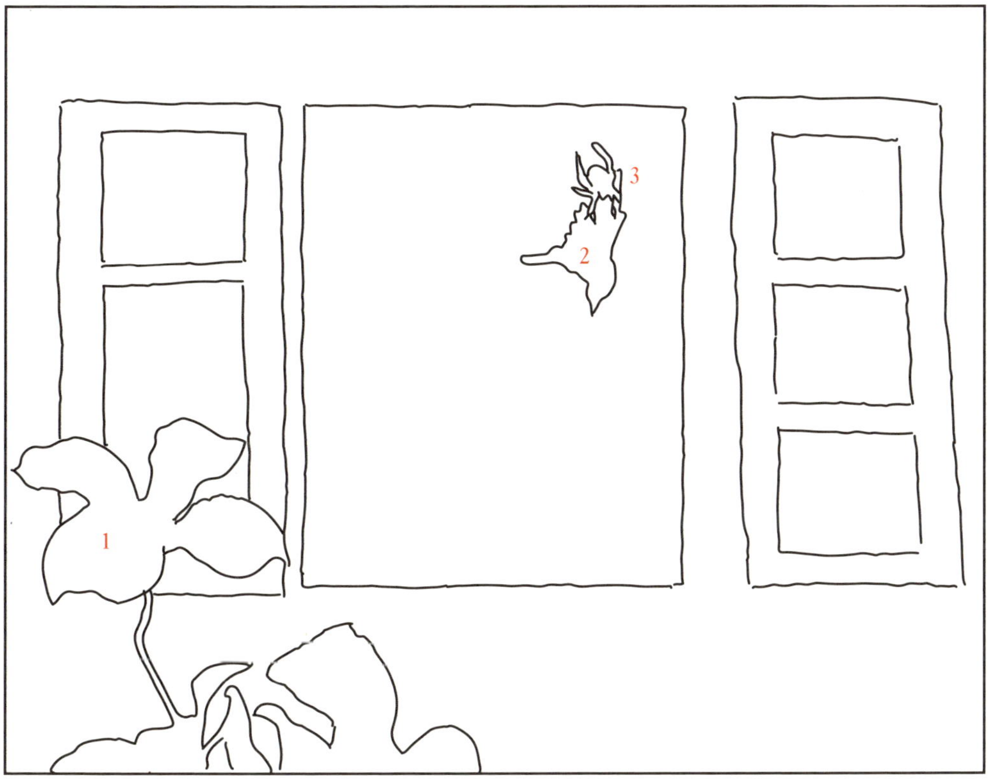

The Window, page 13.

1. Clematis *(Clematis x jackmanii)*
2. Reed Warbler *(Acrocephalus scirpaceus)*
3. Cross Orb-Weaver *(Araneus diadematus)*

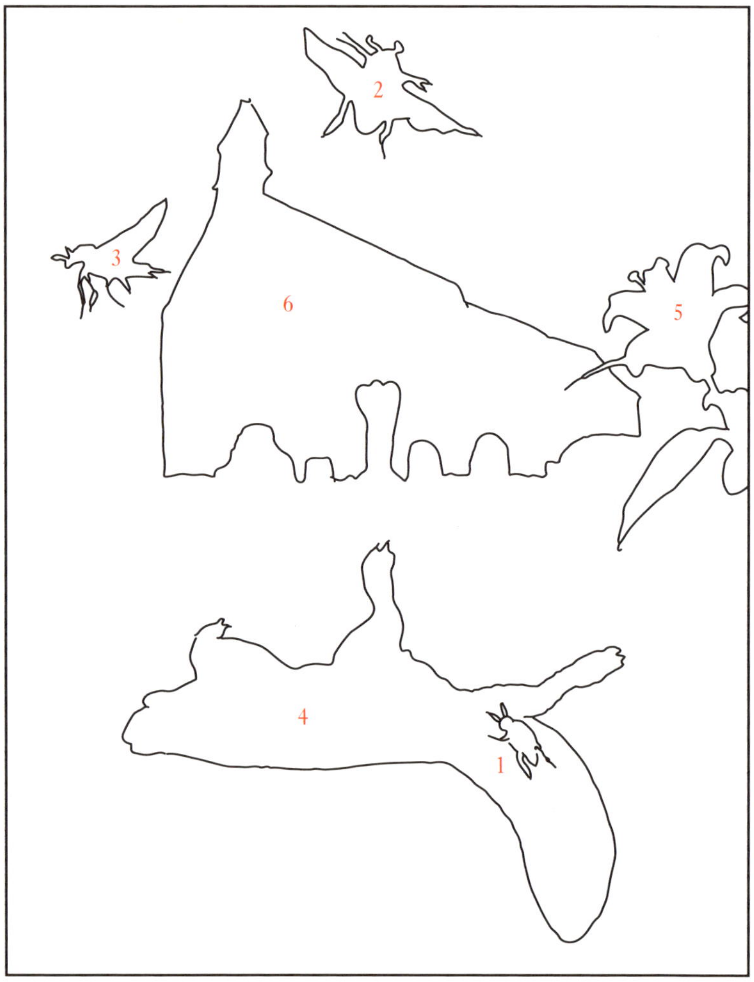

The Circle of Life, page 17.

1. Red and Black Banded Sexton Burying Beetle *(Nicrophorus investigator)*
2. Burying Beetle *(Nicrophorus humator)*
3. Dumbledor Beetle *(Geotrupes sterocorus)*
4. Eastern Grey Squirrel *(Sciurus carolinensis)*
5. Madonna Lily *(Lilium candidum)*
6. Church of St Madoc, Llanbadoc, Monmouthshire, Wales, UK

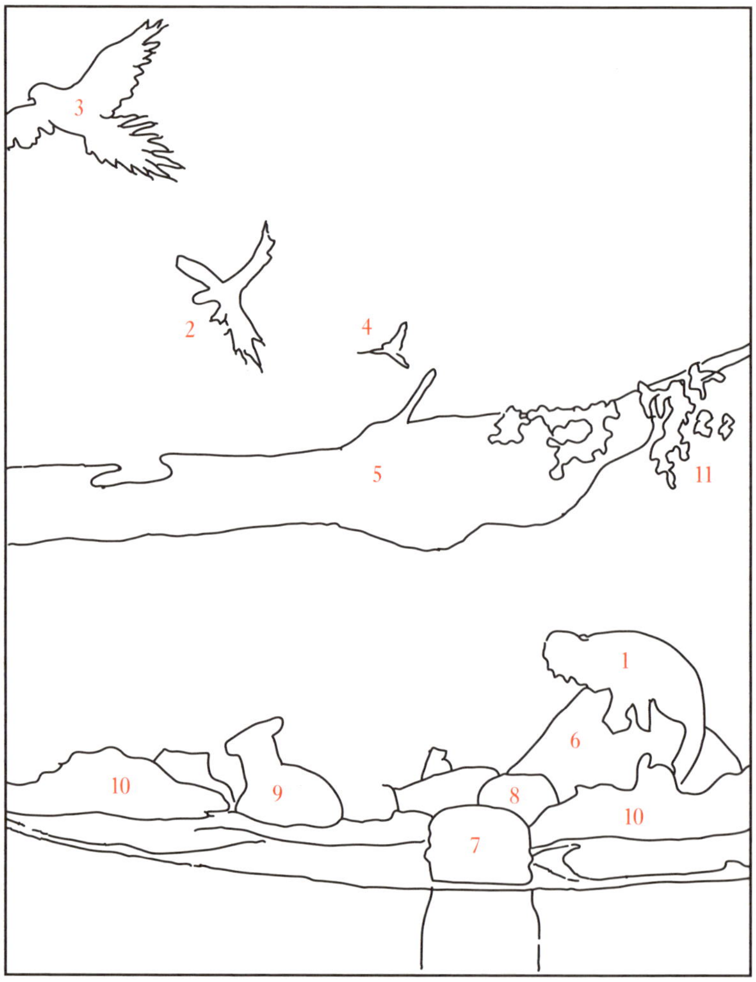

The Sinking of the Brig Helen, page 21.

1. Common Squirrel Monkey *(Saimiri sciureus)*
2. Scarlet Macaw *(Ara macao)*
3. Blue-Gold Macaw *(Ara ararauna)*
4. Hyacinth Macaw *(Anodorhynchus hyacinthinus)*
5. The Brig Helen, lost 6 August, 1852
6. Rum Cask
7. Specimen Jar
8. Perrier-Jouët Champagne Bottle
9. Ethyl Alcohol Bottle
10. Schmutz
11. Humans *(Homo sapiens)*

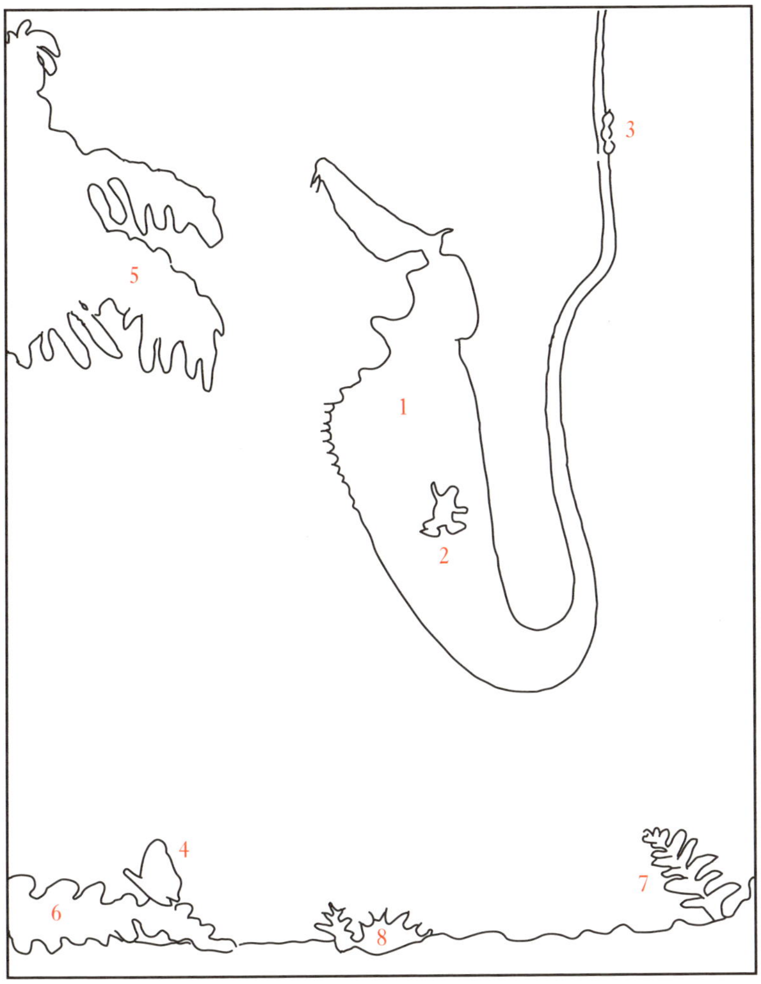

Napenthes, page 35.

1. Pitcher Plant *(Nepenthes rafflesiana)*
2. Matang Narrow-Mouthed Frog *(Microhyla borneensis)*
3. Giant Forest Ant *(Camponotus gigas)*
4. Blue Pansy Butterfly *(Junonia orithya)*
5. Tree Fern *(Cyathea latebrosa)*
6. Fern *(Microlepia todayensis)*
7. Tongkat Ali *(Eurycoma longifoliam)*
8. Moss *(Barbella horridula)*

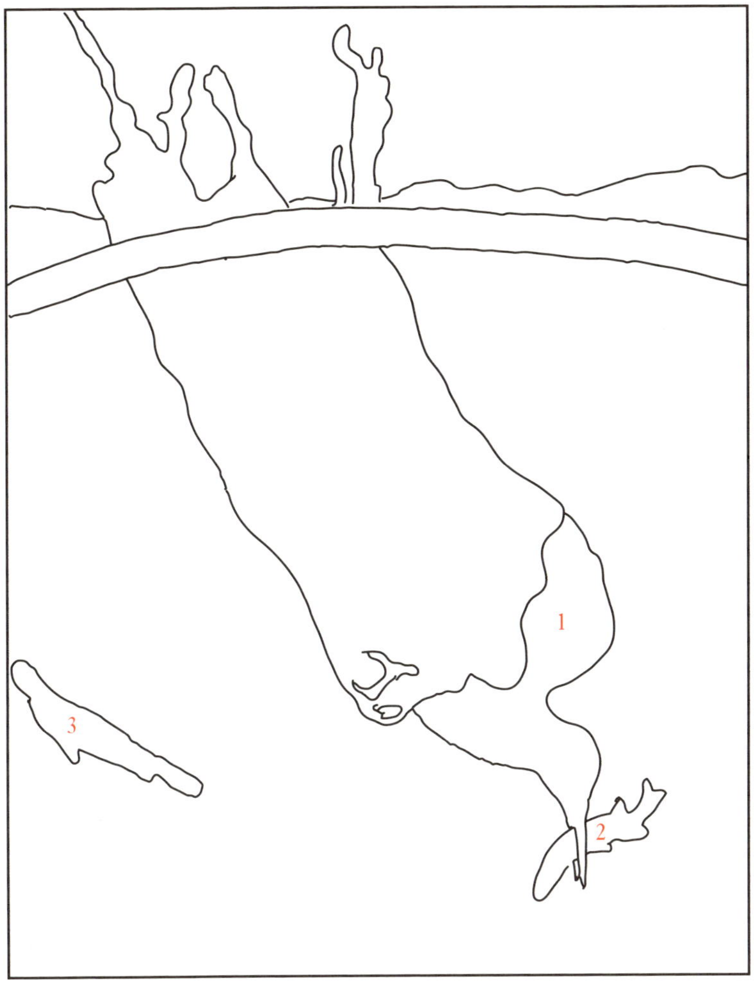

Azure Kingfisher, page 43.

1. Azure Kingfisher *(Alcedo azurea)*
2. Delicate Blue-Eye *(Pseudomugil tenellus)*
3. Platypus *(Ornithorhynchus anatinus)*

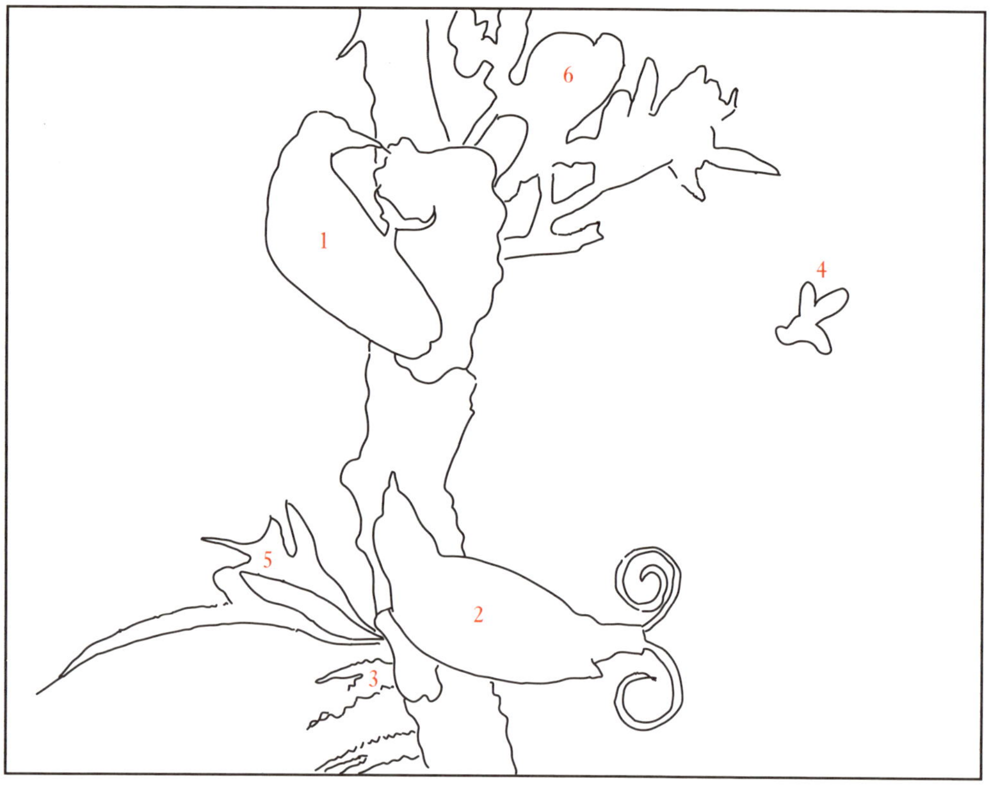

A Striking Coincidence, page 45.

1. Twelve Wired Bird-of-Paradise *(Seleucidis melanoleucus)*
2. Wilson's Bird-of-Paradise *(Diphyllodes respublica)*
3. Fern *(Parathelypteris beddomei)*
4. Neon Cuckoo Bee *(Thyreus nitidulus)*
5. Fern *(Aglaomorpha brooksii)*
6. Ant Plant *(Hydnophytum mosleyanum)*

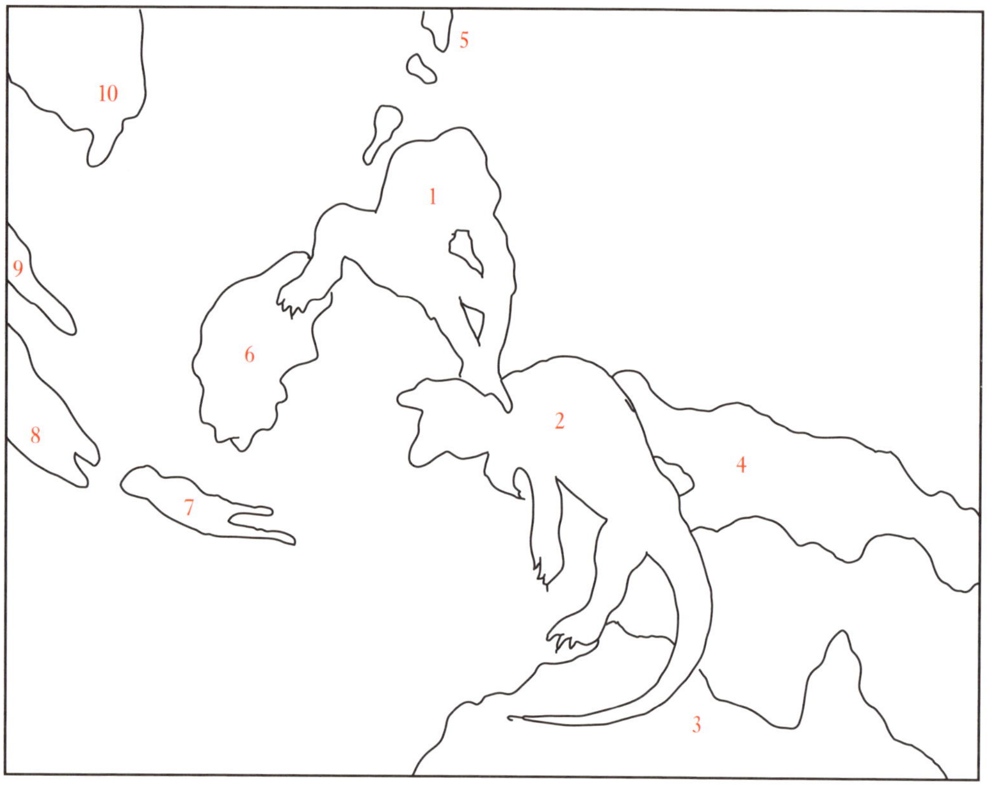

Wallace's Line, page 59.

1. Bornean Orangutan *(Pongo pygmaeus)*
2. Komodo Dragon *(Varanus komodoensis)*
3. Australia
4. New Guinea
5. Philippines
6. Borneo
7. Jakarta
8. Sumatra
9. Malaysia
10. Thailand, Cambodia, Vietnam

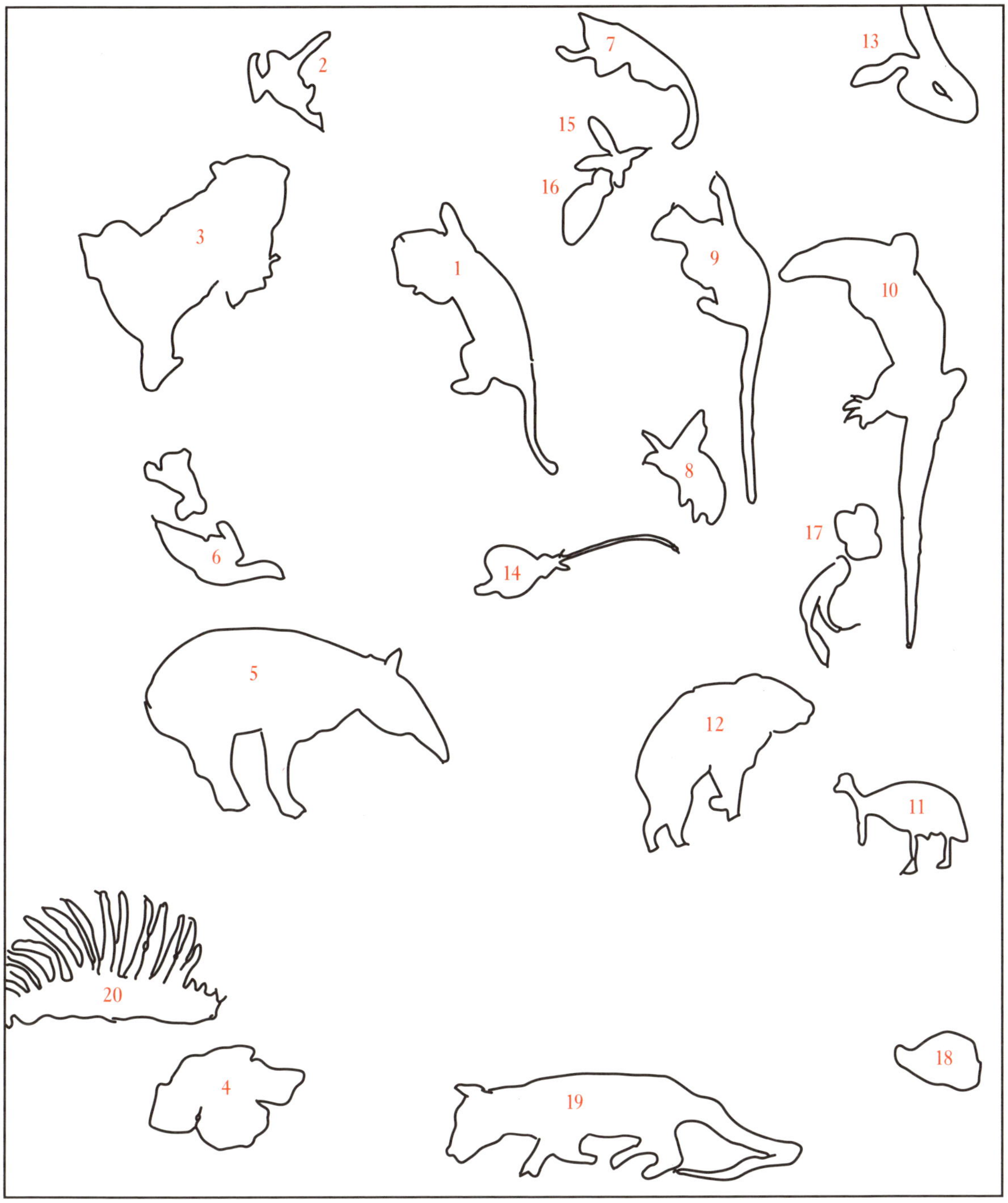

Fever Dream, page 55.

1. Malayan Tiger *(Panthera tigris jacksoni)*
2. Sumatran Orangutan *(Pongo abelii)*
3. Sun Bear *(Ursus malayanus)*
4. Corpse Lily *(Rafflesia arnoldii)*
5. Malayan Tapir *(Tapirus indicus)*
6. Clouded Leopard *(Neofelis nebulosa)*
7. Binturong *(Arctictis binturong)*
8. Greater Bird-of-Paradise *(Paradisaea apoda)*
9. Goodfellow's Tree-Kangaroo *(Dendrolagus goodfellowi)*
10. Komodo Dragon *(Varanus komodoensis)*
11. Northern Cassowary *(Casuarius unappendiculatus)*
12. North Sulawesi Babirusa *(Babirusa celebensis)*
13. Green Tree Snake; blue phase *(Dendrelaphis punctulata)*
14. Flying Lizard *(Draco volans)*
15. Australian Cicada Killer *(Exeirus lateritius)*
16. Cicada *(Gymnotympana leucogramma sp.)*
17. Blue Moth Orchid *(Phalaenopsis sp.)*
18. Marsupial Lion *(Thylacoleo carnifex)* extinct 46,000 years ago
19. Tasmanian Tiger *(Thylacinus cynocephalus)* extinct 1936
20. Aurochs *(Bos primigenius)* extinct 1627

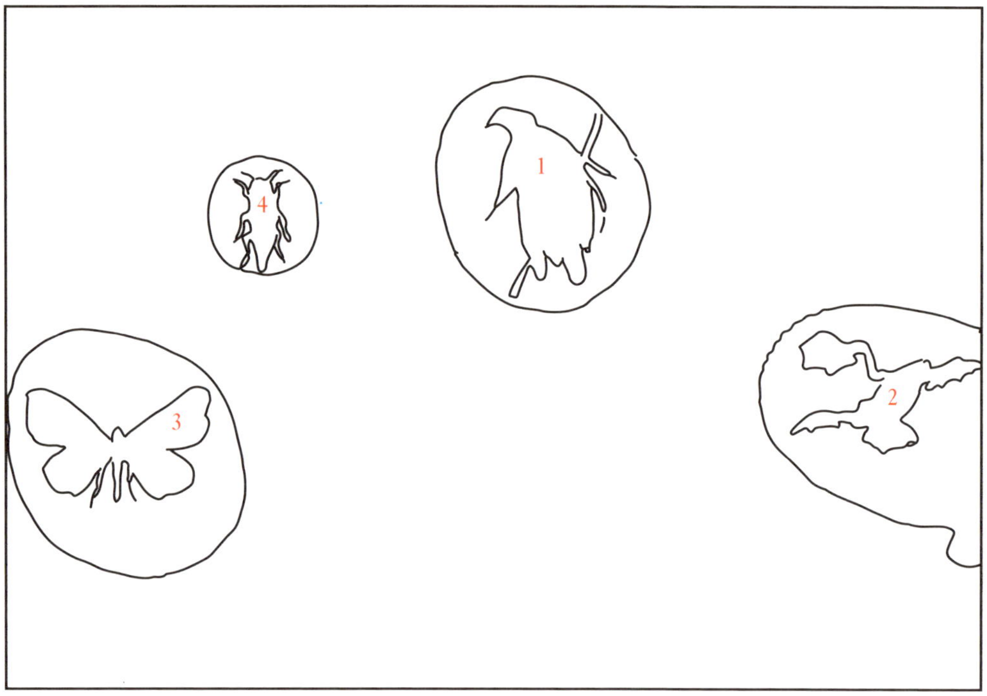

Wallace's Vision, page 61.

1. Wallace's Standard Wing *(Semioptera wallacii)*
2. Wallace's Flying Frog *(Rhacophorus nigropalmatus)*
3. *Cyrtochila wallacei*
4. *Calodema wallacei*

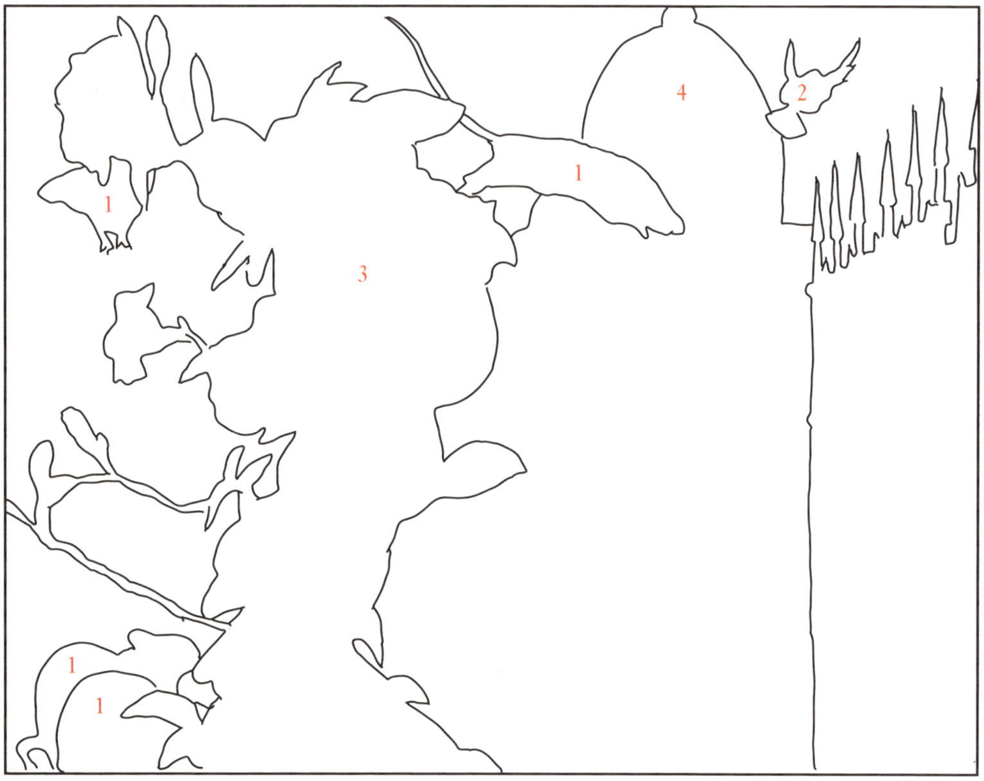

Concrete Jungle in London, page 63.

1. Norway Rats *(Rattus norvegicus)*
2. Rock Dove *(Columba livia)*
3. Clematis *(Clematis x jackmanii)*
4. St Paul's Cathedral, Sir Christopher Wren, 26 October, 1708

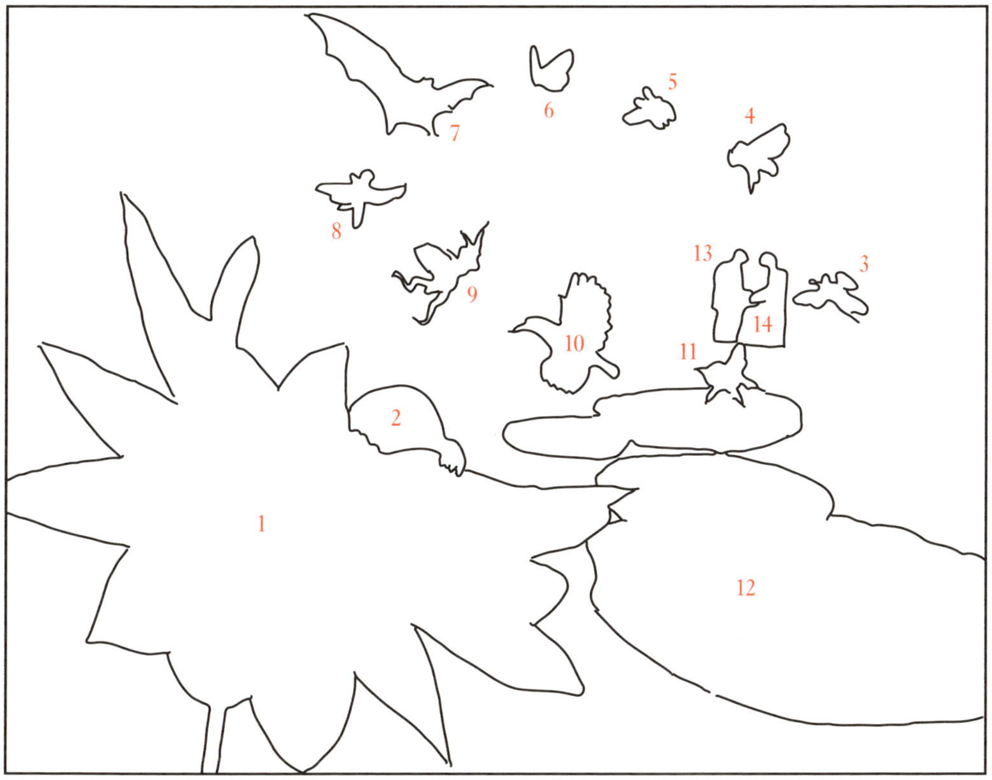

Courtship Behavior, page 65.

1. Victoria Water-lily Flower *(Victoria amazonica)*
2. Sunda Slow Loris *(Nycticebus coucang)*
3. Metallic Green Bee *(Agapostemon sp.)*
4. Orchid Bee *(Abejas euglosinas)*
5. Orchid Bee *(Abelha euglossini)*
6. Common Brimstone *(Gonepteryx rhamni)*
7. Lesser Dog Faced Fruit Bat *(Cynopterus brachyotis)*
8. Portuguese Firefly *(Luciola lusitanica)*
9. Metallic Wood Boring Beetle *(Buprestidae sp.)*
10. Souimanga Sunbird *(Cinnyris sovimanga)*
11. Italian Honey Bee *(Apis mellifera ligustica)*
12. Victoria Water-lily Leaf *(Victoria amazonica)*
13. Alfred Russel Wallace
14. Annie Mitten

This publication accompanies the exhibition:

ALEXIS ROCKMAN:

WALLACE'S LINE.

16 March – 15 April, 2018.

BALDWIN GALLERY
209 South Galena Street, Aspen, CO 81611. Tel 970.920.9797.
www.baldwingallery.com

Alexis Rockman wishes to thank:
Richard Edwards, Kiki Jai Raj, Kerstin Bendl, Carrie Smalley Down
and Sarah Funderburg of the Baldwin Gallery;
Jean-Christophe Castelli;
Tom Baione, Harold Boeschenstein Director of the Department of Library Services
at the American Museum of Natural History;
and special thanks to:
Dorothy Spears.

ISBN: 0-9797936-7-X.

Photography by Adam Reich, New York; John Bonath, Denver; Tony Prikryl, Aspen.
Typesetting and production by Step Graphics, Inc.
Printed by Meridian Printing, Rhode Island.
Bound by the New Hampshire Bindery.
Edition of 750 copies.